● *When baking* a pie, put it in an oven browning bag or plain paper bag. Cut four or five slits in the bag and twist shut. Place on a cookie sheet and bake ten minutes longer than required time. Crust will turn a beautiful golden brown, and oven spills are eliminated.

● *Instead of always* giving your dog a regular bath, rub baking soda into his coat thoroughly and then brush it off. It deodorizes as well as cleans.

● *Oily skin* holds perfume scents longer than dry skin. So, before applying perfume, rub a very thin layer of oily moisturizer or petroleum jelly on your skin and you'll smell delicious for hours.

And there are 2,497 more inside!

MARY ELLEN'S GREATEST HINTS

Also by Mary Ellen Pinkham:

MARY ELLEN'S BEST OF HELPFUL HINTS
MARY ELLEN'S BEST OF HELPFUL
    KITCHEN HINTS
MARY ELLEN'S BEST OF HELPFUL HINTS BOOK II
MARY ELLEN'S HELP YOURSELF DIET PLAN
MARY ELLEN'S 1,000 NEW HELPFUL HINTS
HOW TO STOP THE ONE YOU LOVE FROM
    DRINKING

MARY ELLEN'S GREATEST HINTS

Mary Ellen Pinkham

FAWCETT CREST • NEW YORK

The hints in this book are intended to suggest possible solutions only. The authors and distributors cannot guarantee absolute success. To guard against damage, we recommend care.

A Fawcett Crest Book
Published by Ballantine Books
Copyright © 1990 by Mary Ellen Pinkham
Copyright © 1976, 1981 by Mary Ellen Enterprises
Copyright © 1979 by Pearl Higginbotham and Mary Ellen Pinkham

The contents of this work were originally published in *Mary Ellen's Best of Helpful Hints Book I*, *Mary Ellen's Best of Helpful Hints Book II*, *Best of Kitchen Hints*, *1,000 New Helpful Hints*, and *How to be a Better, Prettier You*.

Library of Congress Catalog Card Number: 89-91904

ISBN 0-449-21714-0

Manufactured in the United States of America

First Edition: March 1990
Ninth Printing: November 1993

Contents

Introduction

The same thing was happening with my helpful hint books as happens with closets. You're looking for the bag of kids' clothes you've put away to pass along or that square dish you use only two or three times a year, and you can't remember where on earth you put the darn thing. So you go look in one closet . . . and then another . . . and then another. It's a nuisance!

Similarly readers would write to tell me that they loved my books . . . but they had a complaint. They'd remember that there was a certain hint about getting the tar off linoleum, but they didn't know in which of my five books to find it. Was it in *Best of Helpful Hints* . . . or the *Best of Helpful Hints II* . . . or it might be in *Best of Kitchen Hints* . . . or maybe in *1,000 New Hints*. (At least they could rule out *How to be a Prettier, Healthier You*.) So they'd wind up going from one book to another to another. Some of them even made up a little index of their own to keep track of the hints they used more often.

I could empathize completely, because the truth is that the same thing was happening to me! When I'd go to look up a particular hint, I myself would forget in which book it appeared.

So, to celebrate more than a decade of helpful hints in print, I decided it was time to "clean my closets." This book is the result.

I've gone through my five hint books and selected the best of the best—the tried and true, most popular hints from each. For the first time, here they are—all 2,500 of them—in a single volume. I know I'll find it useful—and I certainly believe you will, too.

Best of
Helpful Hints
for Baking

BREADTIME STORIES

When you knead a lot of dough
• *Oil hands* a little, and hard-to-knead dough, such as pumpernickle, whole wheat, and rye, will be easier to handle.
• *To keep* the bowl from slipping and sliding while mixing ingredients, place it on a folded damp towel.
• *The tenderness* and flakiness of biscuit dough and pie pastry depend on finely cut cold lard mixed with flour. To keep the fat from melting, handle biscuit dough as little as possible.
• *Dough won't* stick to hands if it is kneaded inside a large plastic bag. Neither will it stick to the bag or dry out.

Rising to the occasion
• *Use water* in which potatoes have been boiled to make yeast breads moister. The texture may be coarser, but the bread lasts longer and is slightly larger.

• *Add half* a teaspoon of sugar to the yeast when stirring it into the water to dissolve. If in ten minutes the mixture bubbles and foams, the yeast is alive and kicking.

• *Or test* by putting one teaspoon into a cup of hot water. If it fizzles actively, use it.

• *Press dough* into a greased bowl, turn to bring it greased side up, and cover; then the dough won't form a crust while rising in the bowl.

Warm enough for you?

• *In a* cool room, set the pan of dough in an unheated oven over a smaller pan of hot water.

• *Or, before* baking, put the dough in a container on a heating pad set on medium. The heating pad makes dough rise perfectly.

• *If the* TV is in use, let the dough rise on top of the set. It's a good source of warmth—and if you're watching a program, you won't forget about the dough.

• *Top of* the dryer is warm, too.

• *Speed up* slow-rising dough by putting the bowl with the dough in a large plastic bag. Fold the ends of plastic under the bowl.

Concerning the upper crust

• *To brown* the sides of a loaf almost as well as the top, use a dull-finish aluminum, dark metal, or glass pan for baking.

• *To get* the dull finish on a shiny new pan, first use it for something other than baking bread or bake it empty in a 350° oven.

• *Your bread* will be crusty if the top and sides are brushed with an egg white diluted with one tablespoon of water.

• *For a* shiny crust, before putting the bread in the

oven, brush the top of the loaf with a mixture of one egg beaten with one tablespoon of milk.
• *A small* pan of water in the oven keeps crusts from getting too hard when baking. Spread warm crust with soft butter for a soft crust on freshly baked bread.

Out of the Oven
• *Cool baked* bread on a rack rather than in the pan. Cooling in a pan makes sides and bottom soggy.

Roll playing
• *Brush a* mixture of one tablespoon of sugar and one-quarter cup of milk on rolls before popping them into the oven for a really tip-top glaze.
• *To keep* rolls hot longer, place aluminum foil under the napkin in your roll basket.
• *If buns* are wrinkled, moisten them slightly and heat in a 350° oven for a few minutes.

Bis-quickie
• *To save* the step of rerolling scraps of dough when using a stamping mold, try this instead when you next make biscuits. Pat the dough into a half-inch thick square and cut it into smaller squares with a knife dipped in flour. Since dough isn't overly handled (as with stamping molds), biscuits aren't likely to be tough.

BATTER'S UP

Keep it light
• *A beaten* egg added slowly to batter prevents the batter from becoming too stiff.

• *If you* must use all-purpose flour for cake, use seven-eighths of a cup for every cup of cake flour called for. Sift twice to make it lighter.

• *To cut* down on cholesterol, for each whole egg called for in a recipe, substitute two egg whites stiffly beaten and folded into the cake batter.

Moister mixes

• *Two tablespoons* of salad oil added to cake mix keeps the mix moist and less crumbly.

• *For a* moister (and fluffier) chocolate cake, add a spoonful of vinegar to the baking soda.

Going bananas

• *Before adding* bananas to cake or pie, dip them in fruit juice and they won't burn.

Orange you smart

• *Use orange* juice instead of water to make a sponge cake more flavorful.

Chocolate "bits"

• *Leave a* square of baking chocolate in the wrapper, then pound with the textured end of a meat pounder if you want to break it in half.

• *Always melt* chocolate in the top of a double boiler to prevent it from scorching.

• *Turn a soup* ladle into a double boiler by placing it in boiling water and using it to melt butter or chocolate.

• *If the* chocolate starts to harden after melting, add enough vegetable oil to make it liquid again.

• *A little* flour mixed into the remains of melted chocolate in the pan will get the last bit of chocolate out of the pan and into the cake batter.

• *Adding a* pinch of salt to dishes containing chocolate enhances the flavor.

Crack-proofing a cake
• *To keep* cake from cracking when baked, avoid overbeating. Too much air in the batter causes cracking.

Preventing holes
• *Holes in* angel food cakes are from air pockets where the stiff batter didn't touch the pan. To prevent this, run a knife in a spiral pattern through the batter in the tube pan, pushing it against the walls of the tube for a perfect cake.

Making additions
• *Heat nuts*, fruits, and raisins in the oven before adding them to cake and pudding batter, and they won't be as likely to sink to the bottom of the cake.
• *Or, roll* them in butter or put them in hot water for a few minutes before you add them.
• *Sprinkle frozen* berries in cinnamon sugar before adding them to cake or muffin batter for great taste and an even distribution.

A taste of honey
• *You can* substitute honey for half the sugar called for in a recipe. Just be sure to also reduce the liquid by one-fourth.
• *Bake any* cake with a substantial amount of honey at a slightly lower temperature than cakes containing only sugar.
• *If honey* has crystallized, set the bottle in a pan of hot water. Heat on stove until crystals disappear. (Same goes for jelly and syrups.)

Watch my dust

• *Use cocoa* to dust baking tins so cookies and cakes won't have that floury look. (Especially good on chocolate cakes.)

• *Or dust* your prepared cake pans with some of the dry cake mix when making a box cake.

Pan plans

• *Trace the* outline of the baking-pan bottom on waxed paper and cut it out. Grease and flour the sides of the pan only and place the waxed-paper cutout on the bottom of the pan. Pour in the batter. After baking, when you remove the cake from the pan, it won't stick. Gently peel off waxed paper while the cake is still warm.

• *Grease pans* with a smooth mixture of oil, shortening, and flour to keep cakes from sticking to the tins.

• *New tins* should be greased and put in a moderate oven for fifteen minutes to prevent burned cake bottoms.

LET THEM EAT CAKE

Done right by me

• *If the* top of your cake is browning too quickly, place a pan of warm water on the rack above the cake while it is baking in the oven.

• *If toothpicks* are too short to test a cake for doneness, a piece of uncooked spaghetti does the job.

• *Take cake* out of the oven and set it briefly on a damp cloth to make the cake come loose from the pan.

• *If cake* sticks to the pan and seems about to split, hold the pan over a low flame for five to eight seconds and the cake will come out nice and firm.

• *A freshly* baked cake that's too high in the center may be flattened to the right shape by pressing the bottom of a slightly smaller pan down onto it. It won't hurt the cake.

• *A cake* rack covered by a paper towel lets the cake "breathe" as it cools. The cake won't stick to the paper towel, either.

Serving them right

• *If a* cake is to be cut while hot, use unwaxed dental floss instead of a knife.

• *To eliminate* mess, freeze your unfrosted cake before cutting it into decorative party shapes. Your cake will slice evenly, too.

• *To cut* a cake without breaking the icing, wet your knife in boiling water before beginning the job.

Tender touches

• *If you* wrap a cake tightly in transparent plastic wrap and let it stand about a day before you serve it, it will be extra tender.

• *To preserve* the creamy texture, thaw frozen cheesecake in the refrigerator for twelve hours.

Refresher Courses

• *When storing* cake, place half an apple in the container along with the cake to retain freshness.

• *Or fasten* a slice of fresh bread with toothpicks to the cut edge of a cake to keep it from drying out and getting stale.

• *Dip stale* cake quickly in cold milk and heat in a moderate oven.

TO TOP IT OFF

Shaving chocolate
• *Curls are* larger when made with milk chocolate rather than with semisweet.
• *When a* recipe calls for chocolate slivers, you can make the finest shavings of chocolate yourself. A chocolate bar and a potato peeler will do the trick cheaply and conveniently.

Correction courses
• *To prevent* hardening and cracking, add a pinch of baking powder when making a powdered-sugar icing. It will stay moist.
• *To prevent* icings from becoming granular, add a pinch of salt to the sugar.
• *If frosting* becomes too hard or stiff as you are beating it, beat in some lemon juice.
• *To keep* fudge frosting soft and workable, keep frosting in a bowl in a pan of hot water. Add one teaspoon of cornstarch for the smoothest frosting yet.
• *Powdered sugar* sprinkled on top of each cake layer before frosting or filling prevents filling from soaking through the cake.
• *Make frosting* smooth by first putting on a thin layer of icing. When this base coat sets, apply a second, final coat. Goes on easily and looks superb.

Other ways to top it off
• *Use devil's* food cake mix instead of cocoa in frosting.
• *For an* easy, delicious frosting, top each cupcake with a marshmallow two minutes before removing pan from the oven.

• *Or add* a little chocolate syrup to a prepared whipped topping.

• *Mix a* fifteen-ounce can of crushed pineapple with three and three-quarter ounces of instant vanilla pudding. Great for topping a lemon or yellow cake.

Hello, doily

• *For a* fast topping for cakes, just place a paper doily with a large design on top of the cake, then dust powdered sugar over it lightly. Lift doily off gently.

Icing ideas for birthdays or Valentine Day

• *Add a* small amount of red, unsweetened powdered drink mix to a powdered sugar frosting. You'll get a pink color and a great flavor.

This hint's write-on!

• *When decorating* on cake frosting, use a toothpick to trace the design or message, then use an empty mustard squeeze bottle filled with frosting to fill it in.

In the bag

• *Before you* fill an icing bag, place it in a tall iced tea glass, with the pointed end extending into the glass. Now when you fill the bag, the icing will go in neatly without spilling.

• *To improvise* an icing "bag," roll a piece of paper into a cone shape so that one end has a smaller opening than the other. Snip the small end with scissors to make a good point. Spoon in icing and squeeze it out through the pointed end.

• *Or use* a plastic bag.

Throwaway cake plates

• *Cover an* old record album with aluminum foil.

Works just as well and you don't have to lug it back home if you're donating a cake or pie to a cake sale.

MY, MY, WHAT A PIE!

Flaky ideas

• *Ice water* used in pie crust keeps the shortening intact and makes the pastry flakier.

• *Lard is* better than vegetable shortening for making pie dough. While butter imparts a better flavor, it also melts easily when the dough is handled and makes the crust less flaky.

Put a stop to sogginess

• *Brush the* unbaked bottom crust of your pie with a well-beaten egg white before filling. This keeps berries and other fruits from making pie bottoms mushy.

• *Or, keep* pie crust from becoming soggy by sprinkling it with equal parts of sugar and flour before adding filling.

• *A nuttier* method is to spread finely ground nuts over the bottom crust. Adds a delicious flavor, too.

• *Or place* pie in a very hot oven for the first ten minutes before you fill it. That will firm the lower crust.

Oatmeal finish

• *Sprinkle about* four tablespoons of quick rolled oats on a piece of waxed paper, then roll your dough over them. They will give fruit pies a nuttier flavor—and extra nutrition.

Staying on top of it

• *If you* brush the top crust lightly with cold water before baking, the crust will melt in your mouth.
• *Brush your* pie lightly with milk before baking to give it a rich brown glaze.
• *Brush your* frozen pies with melted butter before baking. Butter eliminates the dryness freezing causes.

Vent-sures

• *Before baking,* insert tube-type macaroni in the center of the top of the pie so steam can bubble out.
• *Or cut* a paper drinking straw into three pieces and place them in the center of the pie for the same effect.

Saving some dough

• *Make appetizers* out of leftover pie crust. Cut it into strips, sprinkle it with Parmesan cheese, and bake.

Rolling pin treatment

• *Rolling pins* and pastry boards should not be washed, just scraped with a knife or a scraper. This will prevent dough from sticking the next time around.

Facts about filling

• *When fresh* fruit is plentiful and you don't have time to make a crust, just prepare the filling and pour it into several pie pans lined with waxed paper or aluminum foil. Cover and freeze. When you can prepare (or buy) crusts, just pop your pie-shaped filling inside and bake.
• *A spoonful* of tapioca added to pie fillings that contain especially juicy fruits will absorb the excess juice and keep the filling in the crust.

• *Moisten a* narrow strip of cloth with cold water and fit it around the edge of a juicy pie to keep the juice from overflowing.

• *Add a* beaten egg white to sugar used for juicy fruit pies to prevent juice from spreading when pie is served.

• *Or lightly* beat a whole egg, add a little flour, and add it to the fruit for pies.

Good as gold

• *When baking* a pie, put it in an oven browning bag or a plain paper bag. Cut four or five slits in the bag and twist shut. Place on a cookie sheet and bake ten minutes longer than required time. Crust will turn a beautiful golden brown, and oven spills are eliminated.

Mile-high meringues

• *For the* highest meringue, the secret is to add some baking powder to room-temperature egg whites before beating them.

• *For a* higher, more stable meringue, add one teaspoon of lemon juice for every three egg whites.

• *Always spread* meringue all the way to the edge of the pie crust. This prevents shrinking and watery edges.

• *Turn off* your oven and open the door slightly when the meringue is just perfectly brown. The pie will cool slowly and the meringue won't crack or split.

Easier-to-cut meringues

• *Sprinkle about* one tablespoon of granulated sugar over meringue before you brown it.

FOR DOUGHNUT NUTS

Quick and easy doughnuts
• *Use refrigerator* biscuit dough. Just cut a hole in the center of each "biscuit," then fry in hot oil until browned. Drain, add toppings.

Prevent dough from jamming in the mixer
• *If cookie* dough jams the beaters and wears down the motor in your electric mixer, try using just one beater.

Rolling dough on nonslipping waxed paper
• *If you* roll out pastry dough between two sheets of waxed paper, dab some water under the bottom sheet and it won't skid away.

Cutting the grease
• *Let doughnuts* stand for fifteen minutes or so before frying them. They'll be less greasy.
• *Or dip* them quickly in boiling water after removing them from oil. Then drain as usual.

Once burned
• *A few* slices of potato added to the grease will keep doughnuts from burning.

Hard times
• *Stale doughnuts* become breakfast treats when you split them, dip them in French-toast batter, and brown them.

FOR SMART COOKIES

How the cookie crumbles
• *If you* have no cookie sheet or you need extras, turn a baking pan upside down and drop the dough on the bottom.
• *To keep* cookies from burning on the bottom, cool the cookie sheet before reusing. Run cold water over the back of sheet only, then dry it, and bake the next batch.
• *Take cookies* out two minutes before baking time is up and they'll continue baking right on the hot sheet pan—and will never overbake.

A cut above
• *To make* rolled cookies thinner and crisper, roll the dough directly on the bottom of a greased and floured cookie sheet. Cut the dough into shapes and remove the extra dough from between them.
• *By dipping* the cookie cutter in slightly warm salad oil, you get a much cleaner cut. This works especially well with plastic cutters.

Cookie coatings
• *To add* a crispy coating to cookies, sprinkle a mixture of flour and sugar on the pastry board before rolling out dough.
• *Or add* a nuttier flavor by toasting oatmeal topping first. Sprinkle it over a pan and place in the oven, at low temperature, for ten to fifteen minutes.

If cookies (or cakes) won't budge
• *When cookies* stick to the sheet, run the sheet over a gas burner. If this doesn't work, return cookies to the oven for a few minutes.

• *And if* that doesn't work, place a damp towel on the pan and let it stand a while.

Hard times
• *To keep* molasses cookies soft, add a little cream cheese to the frosting. Not too much, or the frosting tastes cheesy.
• *Crumble stale,* hard cookies, save them in a jar, and use for toppings for coffee cakes or for a pie crust instead of graham crackers.
• *To keep* cookies moist, keep bread or an apple in the cookie jar.
• *Stale angel* food cake can be turned into delicious cookies. Shape half-inch slices with a cookie cutter, toast the "cookies" and frost with glaze or icing.

2

Best of Helpful Hints for the Bathroom

Bathroom bonuses
• *Eliminate overcrowded* drawers and messy medicine chests by hanging a large shoe bag on a wall, or behind the bathroom door, to hold toiletries and cosmetics. Childproof it if necessary.
• *Or use* a spice rack placed at adult eye level.
• *Hang a* roll of paper towels in the bathroom. You'll quickly find many uses for it.
• *Put up* a tension-style curtain rod to hold towels for houseguests.

First aid for the medicine cabinet
• *Glue small* magnets inside the medicine cabinet for holding files, cuticle scissors, and other metal objects.
• *Organize medicine* bottles in old ice-cube trays, lipsticks in spray-can lids, and just about anything into small plastic containers.
• *Strip a* piece of adhesive tape onto the front edge of the shelves to keep medicine bottles from slipping off.

16

DISHING ABOUT SOAP

Soak up
• *Use a* sponge to hold soap. When you wash, wet and squeeze the sponge for suds—and there's no soap dish to clean.

Saving on soap
• *Keep a* pint jar with a half cup of water in the bathroom. Drop all scraps of bath and hand soap into it. When the jar's full, run the contents through a food processor for thirty seconds. Pour the liquid soap into a pump-type dispenser and you've got a constant supply of soap. Just rinse the processor in hot water to get all the soap out.

Soap lost its suds?
• *Just prick* it deeply with a fork and you should get as much lather as when the bar was new.

LIGHTEN UP

If you have no interest in deposits
• *Get rid* of hard water deposits on tub and toilet with fine pumice stones that are used to remove mineral deposits from the sides of swimming pools. Pick one up at a swimming pool supply store.

Bowl brighteners
• *Instead of* throwing leftover Coke down the kitchen drain, dump it down the toilet bowl and watch what

happens. After it has soaked a while, the toilet bowl should be sparkling clean.
• *Or, drop* a denture-cleaning tablet into it for a fast cleanup!
• *Or, use* baking soda.
• *If you'd* rather clean it dry, get the water out this way: pour a bucket of water into the bowl. This makes the water flush out, but the bowl won't fill up again. Clean away!

Ring around the toilet
• *Flush toilet* to wet sides. Apply paste of borax and lemon juice. Let set for two hours and then scrub thoroughly.
• *Or, rub* with a fine grade of sandpaper. If the rings are years old, try wet sandpaper (available at hardware stores).

Dampness around the toilet
• *Sometimes moisture* accumulates around the toilet, leaving puddles on the floor. Prevent the condensation by applying a coat of floor wax to the tank.

Rub-a-dub-tub
• *If your* tub is extra dirty, mix a solution of automatic dishwater detergent and hot water. Let it sit for twenty minutes, swish it around, then rinse with cold water.
• *Or use* a mixture of peroxide and cream of tartar. Make a paste and scrub vigorously with a small brush. Rinse thoroughly.

More brighteners
• *Light stains* can often be removed by simply rubbing with a cut lemon.
• *For dark* stains, and especially rust, rub with a paste of borax and lemon juice.
• *To brighten* up a bathtub that has yellowed, rub with a solution of salt and turpentine.

For fiberglass tubs and shower walls
• *Use the* cleaner made for cleaning fiberglass boats.

SHOWER POWER

If your head's stopped up
• *Unclog your* metal shower head by boiling it in one-half cup of vinegar and a quart water for fifteen minutes.
• *For plastic* shower heads, soak in equal amounts of hot vinegar and water.

For shining shower doors
• *A coat* of acrylic floor finish gives new shine to fiberglass shower doors. Makes water spots disappear, too.

IT'S CURTAINS

Washing shower curtains
• *Fill the* washing machine with warm water and add two large bath towels. Add one-half cup each of de-

tergent and baking soda. Run through entire wash cycle. However, add one cup of vinegar to the rinse water. Do not spin dry or wash vinegar out. This method will not work without the bath towels. Hang immediately. Wrinkles will disappear after curtain has thoroughly dried.

Removing mildew from shower curtains
• *To prevent* mildew, soak in a solution of salt water before hanging them for use.
• *Use baking* soda or bleach to remove mildew from small areas.
• *For stubborn* stains on light-colored curtains, wash in above manner, followed by a rubdown with lemon juice.

Smoother ways with shower curtains
• *Shower curtains* will slide easily if you apply a coat of petroleum jelly to the rod, then rub off most of the jelly with a paper towel.
• *Or use* a coating of silicone spray
• *And to* keep curtains from flapping around and tangling with your knees when the shower's on, attach magnets to the corners.

IT'S DRIPPING!

Tie one on
• *If the* drip occurs during the night and you can't sleep, simply wrap a cloth around the opening of the faucet.
• *Or,* tie a string to the faucet, long enough to reach

the drain. Water will run down the string noiselessly until you have time to fix it.

No more waterlogged tissues
• *If tissues* repeatedly get soggy on a damp shelf or counter, you don't need to buy a dispenser. Instead, put little "legs" on your tissue box. Pushpins (the kind that hold message on bulletin boards) do the trick and come in colors that will match any box.

3

Best of Helpful Hints for Beauty Care

YOUR SKIN AND FACE

Keeping skin young
- *Yo-yo dieting* is a no-no: it stretches and relaxes skin, increasing the chances of wrinkles and sags. So try to keep your weight constant.
- *Find a* way to release tension (warm bath, yoga, exercise), since it can cut off circulation and "set" lines in your face.
- *Wear a* sunscreen. It'll prevent pigment changes and brown spots and keep your skin from aging.
- *Even with* sunscreen—try to stay out of the sun between 10:00 A.M. and 2 P.M.
- *Exercise to* get your circulation going. That helps create new skin cells, keeps color in your cheeks.
- *Rest, or* your skin won't get fresh oxygen and nutrition.
- *Don't overindulge.* Alcohol is dehydrating, dilates blood vessels, creating that "Rudolph the Reindeer" nose.
- *Use extra* moisturizer when the room is steam-heated or air-conditioned. Both dry your skin.

Free conditioners
• *Drinking six* to eight glasses of water a day—not including sugary sodas or salty vegetable drinks—to replace what your body eliminates will do more for your skin than any commercial product. (If you do drink lots of soda or vegetable juice, you need even more water.)
• *Also, since* physical activity brings blood to the skin, releasing sweat and carrying nutrients and oxygen, it helps keep skin looking great.

Skin types
• *Unsure whether* your skin's dry or oily? Blend together juice of one lemon, one-half cup of distilled water, one teaspoon of olive oil, and three ice cubes. Let sit until cubes are melted. Then apply to thoroughly cleansed face and wait three hours.
• *Dampen one* cotton ball in the solution and gently wipe across forehead. Wipe a second cotton ball over your nose, and a third on your chin.
• *If all* are clean, your skin is dry. If they're dark, your skin is oily. If they're slightly soiled, you've got a combination.

Oily skin with dry patches
• *People with* oily skin or acne should avoid moisturizers. If you must use one to treat dry patches, find one with minimal oil or you'll make your skin problems worse.

To pick a moisturizer
• *Test moisturizer* by seeing whether it feels hot or cold. Moisturizer for oily skin should evaporate quickly, which would leave your skin feeling cool.

Dry-skin moisturizer should feel warm because it should stay on the skin surface.

Skin chapped? Go green
• *Green-tinted moisturizer* helps cover up red skin (from chapping, colds), while mauve helps disguise yellowish or tan patches, like freckles.

Cleaning your face
• *Doctors recommend* using white facial tissues, since the dye from colored ones may irritate your eyes.
• *Cotton balls* are better for removing makeup than bathroom tissue, which is made from wood pulp and may be harsh.
• *Too-hot water* can break capillaries around nose and cheeks, causing spidery red lines to appear on cheeks and nose. So wash up with warm water.

Getting rid of a blemish
• *Rub a* styptic pencil (used for razor nicks) on a pimple three times a day and it will dry up quickly.

Choosing soap
• *The most* common test of mildness is how easily and thoroughly a soap rinses off. (Exceptions: deodorant and super-fatted soaps must leave a residue.)

A natural scrub
• *Mix equal* quantities of cornmeal and regular (not instant) oatmeal with hot water to make a paste. Apply while still warm. Leave on ten minutes. Rinse

off with cool water. For extra cleansing and tightening, add a few drops of spirits of camphor to the rinse water.

Makeup for problem skin
• *An oil-based* foundation or moisturizer can contribute to an acne problem by clogging overactive pores. You might be better off with a water-based moisturizer.

Quick cover-up for acne
• *Tiny acne* scars can be hidden by applying a dot of concealing cream with a pointed brush before you put on your foundation.

LET'S MAKE UP

Get the most out of your makeup
• *Your foundation* will last longer if you mix it with moisturizer in the palm of your hand before applying.
• *For a* sharp point on lipstick and eyeliner pencils, without as much waste, put them in the freezer for a few minutes before sharpening.
• *If your* blushing powder has broken, crumble and smash it thoroughly. Then keep it in a small, wide-mouthed jar for future use.
• *Stretch your* dusting or face powder by mixing it with an equal amount of cornstarch.
• *Instead of* costly makeup brushes use high-quality artist's brushes.

The best makeup remover
• *Vegetable shortening* (such as Crisco) is an econom-

ical and very effective makeup remover. Massage it into skin and wipe off with tissue.

Eliminate makeup stains on clothes
• *So you* don't smear makeup and stain clothes at the same time, stretch a hair net for bouffant hairdos over your face. Now put on clothes. Keep this net handy for makeup only.

A matter of mascara
• *Don't "pump"* your mascara wand with each application. That forces in air, which dries up mascara. Instead, just pull the wand straight out and apply.
• *If mascara* does dry out, revive it by holding the tightly-capped closed tube under hot, running water for a few minutes. The mascara inside will soften and you'll have more to use.
• *Or thin* it with a drop or two of liquid glycerin from the drugstore.

Put on a happy face
• *If you* have to make a public appearance after a crying jag, use a gentle cleaner. Tears irritate sensitive skin and rubbing only makes it worse.
• *Rinse with* cool water, or wrap an ice cube in a washcloth and apply to puffy areas.
• *If you've* got a moment, lie down and place cotton pads moistened with witch hazel on your eyelids.
• *Drum fingertips* under eyes, lightly press inside corners of eyes.
• *Use a* concealing stick under eyes.
• *Eyes lined* with blue or mauve pencil makes whites look whiter.

If your cheek color tends to fade
• *Try using* the same color in both powdered and

cream or liquid forms. Apply the cream or liquid over regular makeup base, then dust over it with powdered rouge.

To keep your lipstick on
• *Try applying* an ice cube over it. It will "set" the color.
• *Or, apply* a coat of lipstick, followed by gloss, with lipstick on top. This should help the color stay on.

Cleaning a lip brush.
• *Before dipping* it into a new color, dip it in a bit of alcohol poured into your palm. Then blot it before using.

Help for tired eyes
• *Relieve the* strain of close work by stopping every twenty minutes or so and looking into the distance for sixty seconds. That relaxes the muscles used for focusing.
• *Or, look* out to a faraway object, then back to the close work. Go back and forth a few times.
• *And, blink* your eyes for a few seconds, close them tightly, blink a few more times, and rest. This lubricates the eyes.
• *And, close* your eyes for two or three minutes.

HAIR'S THE QUESTION

Don't wash that man right out of your hair
• *If you're* really mad, you may damage your crowning glory. Hair is at its weakest when wet and may break if you tangle it by shampooing wildly. Instead, rub gently, following the line of the hair growth.

For better shampooing
• *Don't wash* hair while you bathe, since soap, residue, dirt, and body chemicals will stay in your hair and make it oily.
• *Very hot* water will not make hair cleaner and may burn the scalp. Use lukewarm water.
• *Don't apply* shampoo directly to your head. You'll have a better chance of even coverage if you pour some into your palm, then rub it on.
• *Most damage* to hair occurs in the drying stage. Don't rough it up with your towel. Instead, pat it dry, then wrap the towel around your head and let it soak up moisture for a few minutes.
• *Blow-dry slightly* damp hair. If your hair is completely dry, blow-drying may damage it.

Homemade dry shampoo
• *If regular* shampooing is impossible, make your own dry shampoo by mixing together one tablespoon of salt and one-half cup of cornmeal. Transfer to a large-holed salt shaker, sprinkle it on oily hair lightly, and brush out dirt and grime.
• *Baby powder* or cornstarch can also be used as dry shampoos. Sprinkle it on lightly, then brush out.
• *To restore* the sheen and remove more dirt, put a nylon stocking over the bristles and continue brushing.

Removing sticky hair-spray buildup
• *Wash hair* as usual, but work a tablespoon of baking soda into the lathered hair. Hair spray will dissolve.

Out of cream rinse?
• *Try a* little dab of fabric softener in a glass of warm water. It leaves hair soft and snarl-free.

Some blues you can use
• *Add a* bit of bluing (the kind used in the laundry) to the final rinse water to prevent gray hair from yellowing.

Get in condition
• *Vinegar rinses* became popular when hair was washed with soap. The vinegar would restore natural acids and remove the dull soap film on hair, thus restoring the shine. Since today's shampoos don't contain soap, skip the vinegar and choose a conditioner suitable for your hair type. It'll replace the natural protective oils that coloring and regular shampooing take out.
• *Mayonnaise gives* dry hair a good conditioning. Apply one-half cup of mayonnaise to dry, unwashed hair. Cover with a plastic bag and wait for fifteen minutes. Rinse a few times before shampooing thoroughly.

Setting lotion
• *A teaspoon* of sugar or gelatin dissolved in a cup of warm water makes a handy setting lotion.
• *Or, for* an extra firm set, use your favorite flavor of Jello. That's right, fully prepared and ready to eat. Use as you would any jellied type of setting lotion.
• *Also, try* witch hazel or stale beer.

For dry, crackly hair
• *If your* hair stands on end even when you're not at a horror movie, try using a brush and comb with fewer, smoother bristles, preferably of wood or metal. They move through the hair faster and cause less static.
• *If hair* still crackles, try rubbing a little conditioner on your hands, then smoothing them over your hair.

• *Or, spray* hair spray or the static-free product used for clothing on your brush before styling.
• *Or, lightly* rub a fabric-softener sheet over hair.

Keep your equipment in shape
• *Hair dryers* need an occasional cleaning. Use your vacuum cleaner and run the brush attachment over the blower end.
• *Electric rollers* should be washed occasionally in shampoo and warm water, and scrubbed with an old toothbrush. Otherwise they'll make your hair dirty.

Storing coated elastic bands
• *When you* buy them by the package, wrap all of them around the handle of your hairbrush. You won't have to go searching for the package or the loose bands.

Keeping track of pics and clips
• *Push roller* pics through a plastic pot scrubber
• *Hang electric* roller clips over the rim of a mug. No more tangles, and the clips hang neatly.

Clogged spray cans
• *Remove the* tip from your hair spray (or deodorant) and hold under hot running water.
• *Or, borrow* a new tip from another can.

DYE IDEAS

Saving the sink from dye drops
• *When using* henna or color on your hair, coat the

sink lightly with liquid dishwashing detergent. No sink stains when dye drips or runs.

Fighting fire with fire
• *If your* tint has stained your skin around the hair-line—or anywhere else—guess what! Hair color removes hair color stains. Just rub leftover tint into the stained area and rinse with water.

If you overdo the dye
• *Flashing a* new color that's as subtle as a fire gong? Don't panic. Buy a "temporary drabbing rinse" in an ash-colored shade.

Banish hair permanent odor
• *You can* get rid of the odor from a new permanent if you apply tomato juice—enough to saturate dry, unwashed hair. Cover hair with a plastic bag and wait fifteen minutes. Rinse hair a few times before shampooing thoroughly.

Believe it or not
• *If you* lighten your hair, it can turn green when you swim in a chlorinated pool. Prevent this by dissolving six aspirin tablets in a large glass of warm water and rubbing the solution into wet hair. The green will disappear.
• *Or*, rub in tomato juice.

TOOTHY MATTERS

Saving a tooth
• *If someone* in the family loses a tooth, rinse it in

water (don't scrub) and pop it back in. Then get to the
dentist, who'll put in a splint to help it reimplant itself.
• *Or, drop* it into a cup of milk to carry to the dentist
for reimplanting.
• *Or, wrap* carefully in a wet piece of gauze and hold
it under your tongue en route to the dentist.

Temporary caps and fillings
• *If you* should lose a cap or filling and a dentist isn't
available, don't panic: you can make yourself a temporary replacement. All you need is two drugstore
items: zinc oxide and oil of cloves (eugenol). They
mix together to form a white paste that hardens
quickly. Rinse your mouth thoroughly first, then pack
the paste into the cavity, clean up the edges, and it
will last for two or three days until you can get to a
dentist.

Preventing canker sores
• *Avoid eating* sharp food like peanut brittle and use a
medium or soft-bristled toothbrush. Physical damage
to the lining of the mouth starts most canker sores.

Squeezing out the last bit.
• *Just use* an old-fashioned clothespin: slip it on and
use as a key to roll up a tube of toothpaste.

SHOW OF HANDS

Condition while you work
• *Two in* one: apply conditioner such as hand lotion
before slipping on rubber gloves and let the heat of
dishwashing help the cream sink in.

• *Or, in* winter, apply conditioner, slip on cotton gloves, and then slip your hands into heavier gloves. Hands will be thoroughly moisturized by the time you unpeel.

A treatment for rough, red hands
• *Place one-half* teaspoon of sugar in the palm of your hand and cover sugar with mineral or baby oil. Massage hands briskly for a few minutes. Wash hands with soapy water and they'll feel like silk.

Itchy fingers?
• *That redness,* irritation, and itch under your wedding band and other rings may be caused by built-up soap trapped underneath. Slide the ring off, rinse your hands thoroughly, and apply a hydrocortisone cream.
• *Or, boil* your ring in soapy water, and don't wear it for two or three days until the itch disappears.
• *Or, pierce* a vitamin E capsule and apply the fluid generously several times a day until itch has gone away.

AT YOUR FINGERTIPS

For extra protection
• *If you're* doing household jobs, take special care of nails by putting a strip of masking tape over each one before you slip on the gloves.
• *Try to* use nail-polish remover no more than once a week. More frequent use can dry out your nails and cause them to split.

Keeping the dirt out
• *Scrape your* nails over a bar of soap before you

work in the garden. Dirt won't collect underneath.
• *Also, wear* gloves when possible to avoid scratches and bruises.

When nail polish gets clumpy
• *Add a* few drops of rubbing alcohol to thin it out.
• *Or, a* few drops of nail-polish remover.
• *Or, cap* bottle tightly and run hot water over it or place it in boiling water. It will then be easier to apply.

Cool it
• *In the* future, your nail polish will always be easy to apply if you store it in the refrigerator. That will keep frosted nail polish from separating, too.

Undercover agent
• *You'll avoid* breaking and chipping if you polish *under* nail tips as well as on top.

Between manicures
• *You can* mend a chip by applying a bit of nail-polish remover with a cotton swab, smoothing the edges of the area. When it's dry, apply a fresh coat of polish.
• *If you've* chipped off some nail as well as some polish, smooth off the rough edges with an emery board before you fill in more polish.
• *If polish* has worn off just at nail tip, apply a thin coat along edges only, then blend the whole thing by applying a top coat.

Get set
• *Oops! Just* finished your manicure and already you've smudged it? Take the polish brush, dip it into a capful of polish remover, and brush it over the smudge once or twice.

Repairing a broken nail
• *Out of* nail-mending paper? Cut a piece of paper from a tea bag to fit the nail. Apply a generous coat of clear polish to the tea-bag paper and press it gently against the break, making sure you also work it under the crack. Then cover with colored nail polish.

An emergency emery board
• *When a* nail file isn't available, smooth nail edges with the striking part of a matchbook.
• *When the* edges of an emery board become worn, trim off about one-eighth inch on both sides and use the inner portion.

To break in an emery board
• *A new* file is often too coarse and rough for your nails. Before using it, rub the coarse side over another emery board for a few seconds.

Techniques for filing and buffing
• *Don't* "saw" with an emery board. Use long, sweeping strokes.
• *Buff from* cuticle to tip. A back-and-forth motion causes heat to build up. That can damage nails.
• *If you* hold your nail file at a slight angle, each layer of nail will be slightly longer than the one underneath. This helps prevent splitting.
• *For longer,* stronger fingernails, make sure that when you file you leave sides straight, rounding the nails at the tops only. Snags occur at the sides of nails.

Caring for your cuticles
• *Don't cut* cuticles. They are nature's way of keeping dirt and bacteria out of the nail base area.

• *To clean* cuticles, insert fingertips in half a lemon and wiggle them around.

To remove stains from fingertips

• *The tips* of your nails are very porous and may be stained by cigarettes, food, cosmetics, etc. Bleach stains away with a lemon half! Wiggle your fingertips in it, then rinse with lukewarm water.
• *Ballpoint ink* or adhesive residue marking up your nails? Rub toothpaste on and watch the stain vanish.

Cure for nail biters

• *Try the* same trick moms use to stop kids from sucking thumbs: a little of that bitter liquid swabbed on your hands. The taste will remind you to stop biting. It's available in drugstores.

GETTING SOAKED

Hang that loofah high

• *Loofahs can* get moldy if they don't dry between uses. If yours doesn't have a loop attached, cut a hole and thread a cord through it for hanging.

If your skin is crawling

• *This helps* cure itchy skin problems. Pour some oatmeal in cheesecloth, tie shut, and hang from the spigot so bathwater runs through it.
• *Or use* the pouch as a sponge while you bathe.

Make your own bubble bath

• *Combine two* cups of vegetable oil, three tablespoons of liquid shampoo, and a thimbleful of your favorite perfume. Beat solution in a blender at high speed for several seconds.

Soften hard bathwater
• *Just add* one-half cup of baking soda.

Bath oil
• *Add bath* oil to the tub only after you've soaked ten minutes or the oil will act as a barrier between your skin and the water.

FOOTNOTES

If your back aches, blame your feet
• *Eighty percent* of the population has foot abnormalities, and about the same number have back problems. Minor foot problems such as a callus or corn, and poor weight distribution, can affect your walk and eventually your back. Maybe your podiatrist can help.

If the shoe fits
• *When you* try on shoes, remember that heels shouldn't slip. Boot heels, however, should slip just a little bit.
• *Shoes should* be a quarter to half an inch longer than your big toe and shouldn't gap when you stand on tiptoe.
• *Arches should* be rigid but soles should be soft enough to cushion feet (crepe, rubber or flexible leather soles are best).
• *Shop at* night for shoes. Your feet swell as much as half a size between morning and evening.

• *Try on* both left and right shoes. If one of your feet is larger than the other (true of most people), you may have an uncomfortable fit in certain styles.
• *Back of* the shoe around the heel shouldn't sag and should be reinforced, preferably with leather.
• *Correctly fitting* shoes can prevent ninety-nine percent of all foot complaints.

Sole food
• *To make* tired feet feel good, soak them for ten minutes in warm water steeped with mint leaves or tea bags.
• *Or, soak* them in a basin of warm water to which you've added a fourth of a cup each of salt and baking soda.
• *Soften them* with warmed vegetable oil, then wrap in a damp hot towel and sit for ten minutes.

Rough stuff
• *After soaking,* rub calluses with a rough towel, massage in two tablespoons oil and a teaspoon of vinegar.
• *Some people* swear that frequent applications of castor oil will make corns or calluses disappear.

Smooth idea for pumice stones
• *Apply glycerin* before using pumice stone. The combination is better than using either moisturizer or pumice alone.
• *Follow a* pumice-stone rub with a thin coating of white vegetable shortening.
• *If pumice* stone gets too soft, buff it up by rubbing across sandpaper or concrete.

Athlete's foot
• *Since warmth* and moisture create the best environ-

ment for athlete's foot, make sure socks are washed after each wearing.
• *Allow shoes* to dry thoroughly between wearings.
• *Avoid deodorant* soaps, since they remove surface-protecting oils and tend to irritate the skin.
• *Cornstarch helps* avoid dampness and reduce friction.
• *You'll perspire* less if you drink less caffeine-containing beverages such as coffee, tea, and cola.

A better pedicure
• *Since pedicures* are best if feet are soaked first, put the stopper in the drain when you take a shower. Feet can soak while you shower.

HAIR TODAY, GONE TOMORROW

Removing leg hair
• *Always shave* after a bath, rather than before. Leg hairs plump up with water and are easier to get off.
• *Shaving against* the grain gets closer results. But if you get ingrown hairs, shave down.

Tweezing hints
• *When tweezers* won't close firmly, wrap both tips of the tweezers with small rubber bands. The rubber grips better and make the tweezers more efficient.
• *Apply one* of the commercial products sold to numb a teething baby's gums to your eyebrow skin to deaden pain.

A tight squeeze
• *If tweezers* are dull, lightly go over the tips with a

nail file, emery board, or pumice stone. Tweezers will be good as new.

SCENT-SATIONAL

Longer-lasting perfume
• *Oily skin* holds perfume scents longer than dry skin. So, before applying perfume, rub a very thin layer of oily moisturizer or petroleum jelly on your skin and you'll smell delicious for hours.

Scenting clothing
• *Instead of* spraying fragrance directly on clothing, lightly spray the ironing board—then press clothes.

If you're sensitive to perfume
• *Spray scent* around the inside heel of your shoes. The heat from your feet will help release the lovely scent. You shouldn't have any problems about direct contact with the scent if you're wearing hose.

Re-using perfume bottle
• *If you* want to keep the bottle that the cologne or perfume came in, fill it with rubbing alcohol and let it stand overnight. Rinse out, then wash with soap and water.
• *Or, use* baking soda and warm water. Let stand overnight.

4

Best of
Helpful Hints
for the Car and Garage

GETTING A GLOW ON

Three ways for washdays
• *On hot,* sunny days, wash and wax your car in the shade or at dusk. This will prevent streaking.
• *A dust-mop* head, worn as a mitten, is great for spreading suds and loosening grime.
• *Or use* carpet scraps glued to a block of wood.

The shining
• *Sprinkle a* tablespoon of cornstarch on the wipe rag when buffing your car and excess polish will come off easily.
• *Or,* for a glittering final finish to a newly waxed car, spray it down with cold water, then towel-dry it.
• *Give windows* and chrome a super shine by polishing with newspaper.

Department of the interior
• *Wipe vinyl* seats and dashboards with a cloth damp-

ened with self-stripping floor-wax cleaner. It removes dirt and also covers scratches and scuffs. Quickly dries to a nonsticky shine.

• *Or try* a solution of three tablespoons of washing soda and one quart of warm water.

• *For those* stubborn tar spots on auto carpeting, apply Spray 'n' Wash; scrub with an old toothbrush.

• *Put floor* mats in the washing machine with a few old towels to get them extra clean.

• *Keep a* box of moist towelettes in the glove compartment for fast cleanups of the steering wheel.

Excuse my rust

• *Chipped paint* spots? Promptly clean the area thoroughly and apply a coat of clear nail polish to prevent rust.

• *Aluminum foil* dipped in cola will help remove rust spots from car bumpers.

• *Or, briskly* scrub the rust spots on your bumpers with a piece of foil which has been crumpled—or use fine steel wool.

• *Or, use* a soap-filled steel wool pad.

• *Or, try* kerosene. (Caution: It's flammable.)

Car body cleaner

• *A grease-cutting* liquid dishwashing detergent will help remove built-up grease and grime from the body of your car.

• *Prewash spray* will remove tar.

Brush off

• *Use a* baby bottle brush to clean those hard-to-reach places on tire-wheel covers.

Cleaning white walls

• *If they're* scuffed up, use soap-filled scouring pads.

• *Or try* one of the prewash sprays and a little elbow grease.
• *Once the* tires are clean, rub on a little vinyl-top wax. They'll look clean longer.

THINGS YOU "AUTO" KNOW

Tires
• *Putting air* in your tires should be postponed until absolutely necessary when the temperature is ten degrees or colder. The valve in the tire may freeze and let all the air out.
• *Test how* much tread is left. Stick a penny in the groove. If you can see all of Lincoln's head, there's too little tread.

Windshield wipers
• *When wipers* begin to wear down, extend their life by rubbing briskly with sandpaper.
• *When dirty* wipers streak your windshield, give them a good scrubbing with baking soda and water.

Battery "cents"
• *Grease one* side of a penny and place that side down on the middle of the battery. Corrosion will collect on the penny instead of on the battery posts.
• *Or spray* the battery terminals with spray paint.
• *You can* also prevent corrosion by saturating each terminal with a carbonated drink.

Oil's well
• *When removing* an oil filter from the car, place a strip of sandpaper between the wrench and the oil filter to keep it from slipping.

• *Keep open* cans of motor oil clean by sealing them with the plastic lids from one-pound coffee tins.

Do-it-yourself oil change

• *Partially loosen* the filter, allowing the oil to drain from it. Then, place a small plastic sandwich bag over the filter and finish unscrewing it. Now, all the mess is in the bag.

Gas caps

• *You won't* forget your gas cap at self-service stations if you attach a magnet on the inside of the door to the tank. The magnet holds the gas cap while you fill the tank. Since the door won't close until the cap is properly in place, you can't forget it.

• *Or attach* the magnet to your car's license plate.

A-PEELING NOTIONS

Removing bumper stickers

• *Use nail* polish remover or lighter fluid. Gently scrape away with a razor blade or knife.

To remove price tag sheets

• *Sponge hot* vinegar onto the price sheets liberally. Scrape gently. Continue applying vinegar until it's gone.

• *Lemon extract* works also.

• *Or, apply* salad oil. Let set for a while and scrape away.

FOR COLD WEATHER

Preventing doors and trunk from freezing
• *Wipe or* spray the rubber gaskets with a heavy coating of vegetable oil or silicone spray. The oil will seal out water, but will not harm the gasket. This is especially good before having your car washed in the winter.

Defogging the inside windshield
• *Use an* old windshield wiper blade on the inside of the window.

Frost foilers
• *Keep car* windows free of ice overnight or for any extended period of time by spreading a sheet of heavy-duty plastic (available at hardware stores) over the windshield. Catch one end inside the door on the driver's side, and secure the other end inside the passenger door.
• *Leave one* window open a crack to prevent frost from building up on the inside of the windows.

Unfreezing a door lock
• *Heat the* key with a cigarette lighter or match. Never force the key. Turn very gently.
• *Or cup* your hands around the lock and breathe on it. The lock will open every time.

When storms threaten
• *Expecting snow?* Park your car at the end of the driveway near the street. You won't have to shovel yourself out before leaving.

Before you get stuck
• *Place a* bag of kitty litter in your car trunk, just in case you get stuck in the ice or snow. It provides excellent traction.
• *Carry a* colored scarf to tie on the antenna to signal help. You'll be seen in the whiteness.

If you are stuck
• *...And there* is no kitty litter, shovel, or sand available: remove the rubber mats from your car and place them in front of the rear wheels. You just might get out all by yourself.

PARKING PRIVILEGES

Keeping the garage floor clean
• *To prevent* oil spots, sprinkle the area with sand or kitty litter. They both will absorb the oil, and you can sweep it up.
• *Or try* to purchase from a friendly service station a sweeping compound that absorbs grease.
• *Or use* a prewash spray to remove grease spots. Spray on prewash and let it stand five minutes. Sprinkle on powdered detergent, scrub with a broom, then hose off.
• *Or soak* with mineral spirits for thirty minutes and then scrub with a stiff brush as you add more mineral spirits. Immediately after the scrubbing, absorb the grease with oil towels or newspaper. Allow concrete

to dry. Then, wash with a solution of laundry detergent, one cup of bleach and one gallon of cold water. Repeat until stains are removed. Caution: mineral spirits are flammable.

Before you sweep the garage
• *Shred some* newspaper and dampen with hot water. To prevent dust from rising and resetting as you sweep, first spread the moist pieces on the floor as you would a sweeping compound.
• *Or try* fresh grass clippings.

Extra storage in your garage
• *Lay a* platform across the ceiling joists and use the space between the ceiling and the roof for storage.
• *Or, shelves* or cabinets can fill the top half of your garage's front wall, since the hood of your car doesn't occupy that space.
• *Or use* old chests of drawers if you have extra floor room, labeling each to indicate if it contains jumper cables, garden tools, etc.

Parking precautions
• *Hang a* tire at bumper height on the front end of your garage.
• *If garage* space is tight, put strips of inner tube, foam rubber, or carpeting on the side walls, where your car door hits when opened.

DON'T LEAVE HOME WITHOUT

Trunk take-alongs
• *Gloves*. *Wear* them when filling the tank at self-service stations, or when changing a tire.
• *An old* window shade. Unrolled, it serves as a mat to protect clothing if you have to change a tire.
• *A bleach* bottle. Cut it in half. The top makes a free funnel.
• *Reflector tape*. Cover a burned-out headlight with it until you can get to a service station.
• *A couple* of coffee cans with reflector tape stripes to use as emergency lights.
• *A squeeze* bottle filled with club soda or cola. Nothing is better for removing grease buildup from the windshield. A must when traveling long distances.
• *Baking soda* and plastic net bags (the kind onions come in). Sprinkle onion bags with baking soda and rub headlights to remove salt residue in winter. You can also use the onion bags to clear insects from headlights and windshield.
• *A broom* with the handle cut down. It's the quickest way to brush snow off a car.

Stash this under the seat
• *A large* plastic trash bag makes a fine emergency raincoat.

TROUBLE ON THE ROAD

Emergency substitutes
• *Use a* hubcap as a shovel if your car gets stuck in snow, sand, or mud.

• *Out of* gas? If you have no funnel to pour gasoline from a can, use a map, newspaper, or paper bag to guide the gas into the tank. Don't light a match.

• *Your radiator* needs water and you're not near a hose? Carry the water in the windshield washer jug or the radiator overflow jug.

Locked out without a coat hanger?

• *Pull out* your oil dipstick, wipe it clean, and push the round end between the rubber door seal and the window. Keep maneuvering until the end catches the lock, then lift.

Light the way

• *Find it* hard getting light just right to see what you're repairing? Attach a bicycle mirror to a flashlight so the beam of light will be directed at an angle, lighting up the area. Seeing "around corners" will be a big help.

If your gas tank springs a leak

• *Plug it* up temporarily with a wad of chewing gum.

5

Best of
Helpful Hints
for Clothes and Jewelry

ACCESSORY-WISE

Buying an umbrella
• *Hold it* up to the light, opened. If you can see through it, you may have moisture seeping through it during a downpour.
• *Count how* many tacks hold the fabric to each rib. Two or three tacks mean a better grade than just one tack. Also: the greater the number of ribs, the sturdier the umbrella.
• *Folding umbrellas* without that automatic opening button feature are very flexible and more windproof.
• *Umbrellas that* open automatically are also more likely to flip inside out than the standard ones.
• *But, before* you discard an old umbrella, remove the little metal tips that fit over each rib and use them to repair any umbrella that's lost one.

Fitting hats snugly
• *Keep one-size-fits-all* hats on this way: measure a piece of elastic around your head and cut to a snug fit.

Weave it through the hat beneath the hatband so it can't be seen.

• *If you're* having a hard time keeping hats that have a shallow crown on your head, sew small grip-tooth combs to the sweatband.

Perk-ups for hats

• *To reshape* an old straw hat, soak it in salt water until it's soft. Then shape it and let it dry.

• *The limp* veil on your hat will perk up after being sprayed lightly with hair spray.

• *Or iron* it under a sheet of waxed paper.

Storage ideas

• *Make a* hat stand out of round oatmeal boxes. Use sand to weight it down.

• *Or use* the inside of the box to hold gloves, scarves, and other out-of-season accessories.

Cleaning leather gloves

• *Use a* hair shampoo with lanolin to help restore the natural oil of the skins.

• *White kid* gloves can be cleaned by rubbing plain flour into the leather and brushing the dirt away.

Keeping gloves in shape

• *After washing* wool gloves, insert an old-style clothespin into each finger

White glove care

• *Add a* small amount of liquid starch to the rinse water when washing white gloves. Starch makes them look new and helps cut down on soiling.

• *Or spray* with fabric protector before you wear them.

To polish metal buttons
• *Here's how* to clean buttons without removing them or getting metal polish on fabric: insert the prongs of a fork between the button and fabric, then clean.
• *Or,* put a cloth around the crook of the button, hold it tightly between your thumb and forefinger and polish away.

For shirt buttons that have discolored
• *Place a* piece of plastic wrap behind the button and rub at the stain on the button with a pencil eraser.

Protect wooden buttons
• *Wooden buttons* may swell and crack when wet, so either remove them from a sweater before washing it or have the sweater dry-cleaned.

No more lost scarves
• *Sew a* small loop of ribbon to the coat lining beneath the armhole and slip the scarf through the loop.

Water spots out of silk ties
• *Rub the* spotted area when dry with another part of the tie.

IN THE BAG

Waterproofing (and dirt-proofing) straw handbags
• *Spray them* lightly with fabric protector. Let the spray dry before using the bag.

To remove mildew from leather bags
• *Wipe them* with a cloth moistened in a solution of

one cup of denatured alcohol and one cup of water. Dry in an airy place. Works for mildewed shoes, too.

Storage solution
• *Store purses* in old pillowcases.

HAIR SUPPLIES

Freshening ribbons
• *After washing* and rinsing hair ribbons, dip them in a cup of warm water mixed with a teaspoon of sugar. Press out moisture on a towel, then iron while damp. The sugar water really gives ribbons body.
• *To press* a wrinkled hair ribbon, pull it across a hot, bare light bulb. This works great with velvet ribbons that an iron would crush.

Drying ribbons and ties
• *Wind them* tightly around a wide glass jar instead of ironing them. They'll dry nice and smooth. Don't worry about keeping a tie in place on the jar—the ends will stick to each other.

UNDERNEATH IT ALL

Slip substitute for gowns
• *Wear a* long, light-colored nightgown with thin straps.

Clinging vine
• *If the* slip is clinging to your legs, turn the slip inside out and you've solved the problem.
• *And if* the dress is clinging to the slip or hose, rub a fresh fabric-softener sheet over them.

Add some color
• *To rejuvenate* dingy white slips and panties, dye them in hot, strong tea until the fabric is a shade darker than desired. Rinse until water runs clear. The color will not wash out.

Delicate matters
• *To wash* fragile lace items, shake them up in a jar filled with warm, mild soapy water.
• *Get wrinkles* out of lace by ironing it on waxed paper.

DRESSED FOR THE OCCASION

Supportive ideas
• *Keep bra* straps from falling off your shoulders by sewing lightweight, thin elastic from one strap to the other.
• *If your* budget can't be stretched—and neither can your bra—buy a bra extender in a notions shop.

Sheer look
• *To get* a very sheer look with see-through blouses, match your bra and slip to your skin color, not to the color of the blouse.

Clinging dresses
• *Run a* wire coat hanger between your dress and nylon slip. This will draw out the electricity and eliminate some of the clinging. Or, use a fabric softener sheet.

FOR THOSE WHO WEAR THE PANTS

Removing hem creases
• *White vinegar* will help remove a permanent crease. Sponge the material liberally with vinegar and press with a warm iron.
• *Try this* trick with lengthening old jeans: the white hem lines will disappear if you mix permanent blue ink with a little water (keep adding water until you get the perfect shade). Then, apply with a small brush. Let dry, and no more telltale hemline.

Removing "pills"
• *To remove* those little fuzzy balls between pants legs, try this: stretch the area as taut as possible over your knee, then rub fabric with a clean plastic-mesh pot scrubber. Don't be afraid to rub hard.

Sticky zippers
• *They will* slide easily if rubbed with a lead pencil.

Renewing a crease
• *To renew* a crease in washable knit pants, squeeze out a press cloth that has been dipped in a mixture of one-third cup of vinegar and two-thirds cup of water. Use the cloth to press the fabric with a hot steam iron.

Blue-er jeans
• *If you* don't want the color to fade from new designer jeans, soak them for an hour in a solution of

cold salt water (two tablespoons per gallon of water) before washing them. Use the cold-water setting for both the wash and rinse cycles.

• *And before* laundering, turn the pant legs inside out to reduce wear from friction.

• *Rejuvenate a* pair of faded jeans by washing them with a pair of new jeans that have never been laundered. You'll be amazed how the dye and sizing that wash out of the new jeans add color to the old ones.

Off the cuff

• *To prevent* the cuffs from rolling up on blue jeans, fold and crease the bottom of the pant legs and secure each with two paper clips before putting the pants in the dryer. Dry the pants separately to prevent snagging on other clothes.

• *Or, if* a denim hem keeps folding up no matter how much you press it, attach a wide strip of iron-on mending material (the kind used for patching) to the inside of the cuffs.

Mud in your eye?

• *Rescue jeans* with muddy knees and bottoms by rinsing them under the faucet and letting them soak overnight in a plastic tub of water with one-quarter cup of ammonia and one-quarter cup of your favorite detergent. Wash them as usual and ground-in mud should be gone.

PULLING THE WOOL OVER YOUR EYES

Sweaters

• *If shedding* angora sweaters are getting your goat,

put them in a plastic bag in the freezer for a while before they're worn.

• *After hand-washing* woolen sweaters, rinse with one-quarter cup of white vinegar in cool water to remove detergent residue.

• *To dry* and block sweaters, take a framed window screen and outline the unwashed sweater in chalk on the screen. After washing the sweater, block it to the outline and set the screen on bricks or across the backs of two chairs. Air freely circulates underneath for quick drying.

• *Fix a* snag by taking a wire needle threader and pushing it through the sweater from the wrong side. Catch the loose thread in the tip of the threader and pull it back through the fabric. If the thread is long enough, knot it to keep it from working loose again.

Patching sweaters with panty hose patches

• *If the* elbows of your sweaters tend to become worn and threadbare, protect them by sewing a piece of nylon panty hose (or stocking) inside the elbows. The patch is soft and sheer enough not to show, but it's strong.

"SKIN" CARE HINTS

Leather

• *Remove ink* from leather by rubbing out the stain with baking soda. As the powder absorbs the stain, it becomes discolored. Reapply the baking soda until the stain disappears.

• *To remove* grease stains, rub with a thick mixture of

Fuller's paste and water. When dry, brush paste off.

• *Using cold* cream is an inexpensive way to clean and soften leather items. Just rub the cream into the leather with fingertips, then wipe clean with a dry cloth.

Fur real

• *Use a* wire brush to fluff up dry, matted trim on fur coats.

• *Caught in* the rain? Shake your fur coat and hang it in a well-ventilated area, away from direct heat.

• *Allow furs* to breathe. Don't cover them with plastic or smother them between other coats in the closet.

• *Put a* pest strip in the closet instead of mothballs. Mothball odor clings to fur and is very difficult to eliminate.

TOPPING THINGS OFF

Gown protector

• *If the* weather's the worst and your gown's the best, try this: cut leg holes in the bottom of a heavy-duty, large-size trash bag, step into it, tuck your gown in and pull it up to cover to the waist. You may look strange en route, but your gown will look great when you're at the party.

GEMS FOR JEWELS

Chain reaction
• *Hang long* necklaces and chains on a small bulletin board and secure each piece with a pushpin.
• *Or, hang* chains on men's tie holders. Fasten the holder to the inside of a closet door.
• *Or, hang* them on small cup hooks that can be easily screwed to the inside of your closet door or to a free wall in the closet.
• *Or, put* them in drinking straws, then fold each end.
• *Or, wrap* chains around a hair roller and secure them with bobby pins.

Angles for tangles
• *When a* small chain is tangled up, try rubbing it between your hands for a minute or two.
• *Or, dust* the knot with talcum powder and untangling will be easier.
• *Or, put* a drop or two of salad oil or baby oil on a piece of waxed paper, lay the knot in the oil, and undo it with two straight pins.

Earring holders
• *Egg cartons*, plastic silverware trays, and plastic ice-cube trays make excellent storage containers for earrings (and other jewelry).
• *Fasten pierced* earrings through the holes of a small button so they won't get separated or lost.
• *Or, line* your jewelry box with foam rubber and stick the posts into the foam.

For shinier stones
• *Here's a* formula gemologists use to clean diamonds, rubies, and sapphires: mix in a bowl one cup

of water, one-quarter cup of ammonia, and a table-spoon of dishwashing detergent. Scrub the jewelry lightly, using an old toothbrush. Ammonia won't hurt gold or silver settings. *Do not* use this formula for cleaning soft, porous stones, such as opals, pearls, turquoise, and coral.

• *Or, clean* gems with a soft toothbrush and Prell shampoo.

• *Or, soak* them in club soda for a while.

• *To remove* remaining soap film after cleaning a ring, dip it in a small bowl of rubbing alcohol, then let it dry without rinsing.

Gold brightener

• *In a* bowl combine one-half cup of clear household ammonia and one cup of warm water; let chains or rings sit in the solution for ten to fifteen minutes. Scrub jewelry with a soft brush and rinse under warm water—with the sink drain closed!

Pearls of wisdom

• *Soak pearl* rings and pins in a bowl of mild soap and water. *Never* use ammonia. Rinse in clear water, with the drain closed, before drying them with a soft flannel cloth.

• *Don't soak* a string of pearls in water. Dampen a soft cloth with soapy water and rub pearls gently until clean.

• *And to* help keep pearls lustrous, gently rub them with a little olive oil and wipe dry with a piece of clean chamois cloth.

Silver solutions

• *Soak silver* jewelry in a mild solution of Dip-It coffeepot cleaner and water.

• *Or, rub* silver with dry baking soda and a soft cloth. Rinse it in water and towel-dry.

• *Or, try* rubbing silver with a soft cloth that has been dipped in fireplace or cigarette ashes.

Super-clean jewelry

• *After the* jewelry has been soaked in the appropriate solution, squirt it with the water jet of your jet oral-hygiene appliance, using clear water. It drives dirt out of the crevices and leaves the jewels sparkling clean. (Make sure the sink drain is closed just in case any gem settings are loose.)

When the ring's too tight

• *Help loosen* a ring when your finger is swollen by placing your hand in a bowl of ice-cold soapy water.

• *Or, rub* hand cream around the band of the ring.

• *Or, rub* soap on the ring and finger.

• *Or, try* holding your hand above your head for a few minutes, allowing the blood to drain.

An ounce of prevention

• *Don't lose* that pin! Cut a wide rubber band to a length of one-half inch. Push the pin through clothing, but before locking it, put the pin through the rubber. If the lock opens, the rubber band will prevent the pin from falling off.

• *Be extra* cautious when attaching charms to a charm bracelet. Place a drop of clear glue on the small ring opening to prevent loss.

Jewelry restringing

• *Use the* finest fishing line to restring a broken neck-lace. The line is firm enough so that you do not need a needle, but soft enough to hand string beautifully.

• *When restringing* beads of graduated sizes, tape a

strip of cellophane tape (sticky side up) on a smooth surface. Arrange beads in order before restringing.

SHEER BRILLIANCE

Testing . . . just testing
• *Before buying* hose, if you want to test the shade, try it over the inside of your forearm, not the back of your hand. The color will be truer, since your forearms (like your legs) get less exposure to the sun.
• *Fluorescent light* in shops may add a greenish blue cast. Try if possible to test colors in natural light.

Clear solution
• *Instead of* storing hose or nylon knee-highs in a dresser drawer, put each pair in a small plastic sandwich bag. It's easy to pick out the right color and the bags are snag-proof.

Longer-lasting panty hose
• *Before you* ever wear a new pair of hose, they should be frozen first. No kidding, they'll last longer if you wet them thoroughly, wring out gently, place in a plastic bag and toss in the freezer. Once frozen, thaw in bathtub and then hang to dry. It's a wild and crazy hint, but it works for me.
• *Or, starch* them very, very lightly. This helps resist runs and they'll also go on easily.
• *Liquid fabric* softener, because it lubricates the fibers, adds life to hosiery. Keep some handy in a leftover dishwashing-detergent squirt bottle and add a dash to the final rinse.

Wash and dry

• *Panty hose* bounce back into shape if you rinse them in a basin of warm water and three tablespoons of vinegar.

• *To quickly* dry panty hose, hang them on a towel rod and blow them dry with a hair dryer.

Running around

• *Apply hair* spray or rub with a wet bar of soap to stop a run.

• *The old* standby—clear nail polish—is still an excellent remedy.

If you do get a run

• *Cut the* damaged leg off the panty hose and pair it with another one-legged pair.

• *Cut the* labels off the ones with runs and you'll know which ones to wear. Wear the good ones with skirts and the others under pants.

New lease on life

• *When a* pair of panty hose becomes nubby but is still wearable, turn it inside out. You have a new pair.

• *Same goes* for tights.

• *Two similar* stockings of different shades can easily be made into a matching pair. Drop them into boiling water and add a couple of tea bags. Remove them when the water has cooled and they will match perfectly. The more tea bags you use, the darker the shade will be.

Keep 'em up

• *If they're* falling down, cut the elastic bands off an old pair of knee-high nylons, slide them up over the socks to the top, and fold down once along the cuff.

Teaching old hose new tricks
• *Stuff sagging* upholstery or pillows.
• *Wrap around* wire coat hangers to keep clothes from slipping off.
• *Wrap a* package if you're out of twine. Snip legs off and tie around the box. Cut the knot ends short.
• *They're the* greatest to tie up stacks of newspaper.
• *Stuff a* water bottle and use as a kneeling pad.
• *Stuff a* toe with catnip, and you've got a toy for your kitty.
• *Stuff with* mothballs and hang in a closet or stow in a cedar chest.
• *Store plant* bulbs in the foot and hang them high and dry.
• *Use them* in the garden to tie up garbage bags, trees, plants, and shrubs.
• *Use as* a strainer or trap on the skimmer basket of a swimming pool.

THESE "SHOE" ARE GREAT HINTS

Polished to perfection
• *Soften hardened* shoe polish by heating the metal container in a pan of hot water.
• *A clean* powder puff is a terrific shoe-polish applicator.
• *And when* your shoe brush becomes caked with polish, soak it for one-half hour in a solution of warm, sudsy water and a few teaspoons of turpentine. Rinse and let dry.
• *Use both* liquid and cake-wax polishes. The liquid polish covers up scuff marks; the wax polish adds the

shine. Apply the liquid first, let it dry, then apply the cake-wax polish and buff. It makes a big difference.

Shine on the job

• *For that* quick polish at the office, rub a little dab of hand cream on each shoe and buff thoroughly.

Scuff cover ups

• *Cover scuffs* on white shoes with white typewriter correction fluid (available at stationery stores) before polishing.

• *Acrylic paint* or paint used to touch up car nicks is helpful in restoring badly scuffed shoes.

• *Light scuff* marks can be removed from most light-colored leather shoes with an art-gum eraser (available at stationery stores).

• *Scrub scuff* marks on silver and gold shoes with a toothbrush and white toothpaste; the marks will vanish.

To boot

• *Make your* own boot tree: tie together two or three empty paper-towel tubes; stand them in the legs of your boots to hold them upright.

• *Or, use* large soda bottles or rolled-up newspapers or magazines.

• *Or, hang* them up with a clamp-type pants hanger.

• *Rubber boots* will slip on and off easily if you spray the insides with furniture polish and wipe them clean.

For you, pardner

• *Spray the* inside of cowboy boots with silicone spray (available at hardware stores) and you'll slip in and out of them without a struggle. (This also holds down foot odor.)

• *To prevent* cowboy boots from turning up at the

toes, clip the sole at the tip of the toe to a clipboard, then weigh the heels down with a few heavy cans inside the boot.

On the canvas
• *Spray new* canvas or rope-trimmed shoes with a fabric protector to keep them looking new.
• *Keep white* tennis shoes looking new by spraying heavily with starch.
• *Clean grimy* tennis shoes by rubbing them with a wet, soap-filled scouring pad.
• *After they've* been washed, push a smooth stone into each to help them keep their shape.
• *Or, once* they've been washed and dried, stuff the toes with paper towels, then dab undiluted liquid starch on the toes and let dry. They'll keep their shape and wear longer.
• *When the* crepe sole of a washable canvas shoe becomes loose, spread clear silicone glue (available at paint and hardware stores) between the sole and the shoe. Hold them together with rubber bands or tape for twelve to twenty-four hours.

For your blue (and other color) suedes
• *Remove scuff* marks or rain spots from suede by rubbing with very fine sandpaper.
• *Keep those* suede shoes looking like new: rub thoroughly with a dry sponge after they've been worn.
• *Steam-clean* suede the easy way. First remove all dirt with a suede brush or dry sponge, then hold shoes over a pan of boiling water. Once the steam raises the nap, stroke the suede with a soft brush in one direction only. Allow the shoes to dry completely before wearing them.

Tied down

• *Coat eyelets* of white shoes with a clear nail polish to prevent discoloration of laces.

• *If the* plastic tip comes off the end of the shoelace, dip the frayed end in glue and shape to a point. Let dry before using.

• *Leather shoelaces* stay tied longer when a few drops of water are sprinkled on the knot.

• *To untie* muddy or wet knots from shoes, use a crochet hook.

Shoe deodorizers, homemade

• *Cut an* old sock in half at the heel. Sew or tie closed one end of the top piece to make two pouches, fill the pouches with one-eighth cup of baking soda, then tie the pouches closed. Place one pouch in each shoe to help absorb shoe odors and keep closet smelling fresh.

• *Or put* some baking soda in the shoe.

• *One other* solution to bad-smelling shoes: buy extra pairs and give each a longer airing out between wearings. You'd be amazed what a difference that can make.

New shoes

• *Sandpaper the* soles of new shoes to make them less slippery.

• *Or rub* the soles across the sidewalk before wearing them.

• *Or rub* a little scouring powder on the sole.

Wet shoes

• *Use a* solution of equal amounts of vinegar and water to remove salt from shoes and boots.

• *Coat rain-soaked* shoes with saddle soap while they

are still wet. Stuff the inside with black-and-white newspaper and leave the soap on for at least twenty-four hours.

Drying tips

• *Dry shoes* away from direct heat to prevent stiffness.

• *A sure* way to dry children's boots fast: drop the hose of a portable hair dryer into the boot. Let it run until the boot is completely dry.

Where to put those dripping wet boots

• *Save your* floors from getting wet. Put a couple of those plastic flats you find in plant shops and stand boots on them at the door. The flats are easy to rinse off later.

• *Put a* box of kitty litter at the door to absorb the moisture from wet boots.

Shoes too tight?

• *Saturate a* cotton ball with rubbing alcohol and rub the tight spot on the inside of the shoe. Put both shoes on immediately and walk around. Repeat until the tight shoe feels comfortable.

• *Or, purchase* a shoe-stretching product from your shoe-repair shop.

OUT OF THE CLOSET

When it's too humid

• *To help* prevent dampness in a closet, fill a coffee can with charcoal briquettes. Punch holes in the cover and place the container on the closet floor. For larger closets, use two or three one-pound coffee cans.

• *You can* also cut down on dampness by wrapping and tying together twelve pieces of chalk and hanging them in your closet.

On the scent
• *For sweet-smelling* closets, hang an old nylon stocking filled with cedar chips in the closet. This also serves as an excellent moth repellent.

Uncrowding closets
• *File notches* about an inch apart on a wooden clothes pole. Notches will keep clothes on hangers from being jammed too close together and wrinkling.

Pants hangers that have lost their grip
• *Wind rubber* bands around each end of both sides of the hangers.
• *Or, put* a strip of adhesive-backed foam insulation on the hangers.

BOX STORAGE

Cardboard cartons
• *If you* live in a humid climate and plan to pack away clothing in corrugated boxes, first coat the box and cover with thinned shellac to keep out moisture.

Odor remover
• *If a* trunk smells musty, place a coffee can filled with kitty litter deodorizer inside the trunk overnight.

Help prevent moth damage
• *In addition* to mothballs, put whole cloves in pockets of woolen coats or in bags with sweaters

when storing for the off-season. They help prevent moth damage and have a nice spicy odor.
• *Before storing* blankets for the summer, wash them and add two cups of mothballs to the rinse water.

Labeling plastic bins
• *The design* of some plastic storage bins for toys, clothing, etc., permits no easy way to label the contents. Try cutting a slit in a toilet paper roll, writing the contents on it (or adding an actual label to it, if you want to dress things up a bit), then slipping the slit roll over the front edge of the bin. Also—when contents are shifted around, labels can easily be moved along with them.

6

Best of Helpful Hints for Cooking

WHAT'S FOR BREAKFAST

Lumpless cereal
• *Prevent lumps* when cooking hot cereal by starting with cold water instead of boiling water. You'll find the texture much smoother.
• *Or, use* a wooden spoon and pour the cereal onto the back of it while mixing it into the water.

Pancake makeup
• *Add fruit-flavored* yogurt drink (available in the yogurt section of the supermarket) to the pancake mix. Substitute it for the liquid indicated in the recipe, then add milk to thin the batter to the desired consistency.
• *For the* lightest pancakes ever, replace liquid in pancakes and waffles with club soda. Use up all the batter; do not store. Close windows before cooking or pancakes may float out.
• *Store extra* pancakes or waffles in plastic bags in your freezer. Just pop them in the toaster to heat.

Syrup substitutes
• *Add a* bit of water and dab of butter to any fruit jelly and heat in a saucepan.

• *Or add* several tablespoons of your favorite jam or preserves to one cup of light corn syrup, then heat.
• *Or, use* the syrup from canned fruit. Thicken it with a little cornstarch, heat, and serve.

Crepes with class

• *For lighter* crepes, use three parts skim milk and one part water. The crepe is heavier when you use only milk or light cream as liquid.
• *For perfectly* thin and tender crepes, use just enough batter to cover the bottom of the pan. A thin, thin layer is the secret to success.

STARTING OFF

Out of the freezer, onto the hors d'oeuvres tray
• *Defrost cheese-* or meat-filled tortellini and cook them according to the directions on the package. Toss them with a light garlic dressing, sprinkle with Parmesan, and serve with toothpicks.
• *Defrost a* box of spinach soufflé, then spoon into large, fresh mushroom caps until filled but not overflowing. Bake in a 375° oven for about fifteen minutes. Recipe yields about two dozen.

IN THE SOUP

Make it clear
• *Adding two* or three eggshells to your soup stock and simmering it for ten minutes will help clarify the broth.

• *Or strain* stock through clean nylon hose or a coffee filter.

For vegetable soups

• *When making* split-pea soup, add a slice of bread when you start cooking the liquid and peas together. This will keep the peas from going to the bottom and burning or sticking.

• *To prevent* curdling of the milk or cream in tomato soup, add the tomato soup to the milk rather than vice versa.

• *Or first* add a little flour to the milk and beat well.

De-fatting the soup

• *If time* allows, the best method is to refrigerate the soup until all the fat hardens on top.

• *Or wrap* ice cubes in a piece of cheesecloth or paper towel and skim over the top.

• *Lettuce leaves* also absorb fat. Place a few in the pot and remove them with the fat that clings to them

Make no bones about it

• *Put soup* bones and all other ingredients that will be removed from the broth into a vegetable steamer. Just lift out the steamer when the soup's done.

• *If you're* using soup bones, use an acidic ingredient such as tomatoes, vinegar, or lemon juice. The acid will draw the calcium from the bones into the soup.

An idea for leftover chicken soup

• *Use it* instead of oil to stir-"fry" favorite vegetables.

IN THE LUNCH PAIL

Unsoggy sandwiches
• *Keep sandwiches* from becoming limp and soggy by spreading butter or margarine all the way to the crusts of the bread before adding filling.

Portable shakers
• *Make portable* salt-and-pepper shakers by cutting straws, filling with şalt and pepper, and twisting ends up.

Dressing on the run
• *Small plastic* pill containers with snap-on lids are great for holding salad dressing, catsup, or mustard.
• *Empty, clean* film canisters serve the same purpose.

SALAD DAYS

Freshenin' up
• *To remove* the core from a head of lettuce, hit the core end once against the counter top sharply. The core will then twist out. This method also prevents the unsightly brown spots that result from cutting into lettuce.
• *Fit the* bottom of a colander with a nylon net and use as a receptable for salad ingredients. When batch is washed, take the net out by the edges, squeeze out the water, and you've got everything handy for the salad bowl.
• *To prevent* soggy salads, place an inverted saucer in the bottom of the salad bowl. The excess liquid drains

off under the saucer and the salad stays fresh and crisp.

Salad Do's
• *To keep* a wooden salad bowl from becoming sticky, wash and dry it thoroughly, then rub the bowl well, inside and out, with a piece of waxed paper.
• *Or rub* the inside of a wooden bowl with a piece of walnut meat. This also removes scratches.

DAIRY DIARY

Make your own "condensed" milk
• *Mix one* and one-eighth cups of dry milk powder and one-half cup of warm water in a double boiler. Stir in a three-quarter cup of granulated sugar and stir over gently boiling water until sugar is dissolved. Remove mixture from double boiler and milk is ready.

Wine in dairy dishes
• *Add wine* first to dishes that contain cream, eggs, or butter, and they won't curdle.

Low-calorie topping substitute
• *Beat an* egg white and a sliced banana with an egg beater until stiff. Mix about four minutes, or until banana is completely dissolved.

EAT YOUR VEGETABLES

Beets
• *To keep* beets red, cook them whole with two inches of stem.
• *Also add* a few tablespoons of vinegar to the cooking water to prevent fading.

Broccoli
• *A slice* or two of stale bread in cooking water minimizes the cooking odor of broccoli. Skim the bread from the surface after cooking. This works with cabbage, too.
• *Broccoli stems* can be cooked in the same length of time as the flowerets if you make X incisions from top to bottom through stems.

Cabbage
• *To reduce* odor while cooking cabbage, place a small cup of vinegar on the range.
• *Or add* a wedge of lemon to the pot.
• *To remove* cabbage leaves more easily for stuffed cabbage recipes, place the entire cabbage in water and bring it to a boil. Remove head, drain, and then pull off the leaves that have softened. Return the rest of the cabbage head to the water and repeat until all the leaves are soft enough to peel off.
• *To avoid* buying a cabbage with a strong flavor and a coarse texture, be sure no separate leaves are growing from the main stem below the head.
• *A wooden* pick or two inserted through the cabbage wedge will hold the leaves together during cooking.

Carrots
• *Remove tops* of carrots before storing in the refrig-

erator. Tops drain carrots of moisture, making them limp and dry.

Cauliflower
• *To keep* a cauliflower bright white, add a little milk during cooking.
• *Cauliflower odor* is almost eliminated if you drop a few unshelled walnuts into the pot. Also works for cabbage odors.

Corn on the Cob
• *To remove* corn silk: Dampen a toothbrush and brush downward on the cob of corn.
• *Or use* a damp paper towel or terrycloth. Every strand should come off.
• *Drop ears* of corn into a basket used for french frying potatoes, then immerse them in a pot of boiling water. You won't have to fish around for the ears: just lift out the basket when corn is done.
• *And don't* waste butter: use a pastry brush to spread melted butter on corn. A celery stalk or piece of buttered bread also makes an instant pastry brush.
• *Or, for* hot buttered corn for a large group, fill a large quart jar with hot water and sticks of butter. When butter melts and floats to top, dip in the cobs and pull out slowly. The butter covers the corn perfectly.

Lettuce
• *Pass up* light-colored salad greens for darker ones and you'll be getting more nutrition for your dollar. For example, use kale or spinach instead of iceberg lettuce.
• *If your* family eats only "token" vegetables like corn, green beans, and iceberg lettuce, they probably aren't getting enough vitamin A.

• *Use lettuce* leaves instead of tortillas for a delicious low-cal burrito. Fill with chopped vegetables.

Mushrooms

• *Store mushrooms* in refrigerator in a brown paper bag—never a plastic one. Otherwise they become slimy. Paper lets the mushrooms breathe while holding in the humidity that keeps them fresh.

• *Use an* egg slicer to slice fresh mushrooms quickly and uniformly.

• *Before your* extra mushrooms go bad, puree them in your blender with a little liquid—water, beef, or chicken broth—and pour them into ice-cube trays and freeze. Remove when solid and store in freezer in plastic bags. Great for soups, stews, or sauces.

• *Keep mushrooms* white and firm when sautéeing them by adding a teaspoon of lemon juice to each quarter pound of melted butter.

• *If mushrooms* are too wet when cooking, they release too much moisture and steam instead of browning. Stirring the mushrooms with a long-handled fork and keeping fat very hot keeps steam from building up.

Onions

• *Keep onions* whole when cooking them by cutting a small cross, one-quarter inch deep, in the stem end.

• *Or, punch* a hole through the center of each onion with a metal skewer.

• *Or, stab* the peeled onion with a fine-tined fork about halfway through to the center. The onion should keep its shape.

• *Once an* onion has been cut in half, rub the leftover cut side with butter and it will keep fresh longer.

• *To make* onions less strong, slice and separate them

into rings, then soak them in cold water for one hour. (Mild onions are great for salads).

• *Shed fewer tears:*

> •*Cut the* root end of the onion off last.
> •*Refrigerate onions* before chopping.
> •*Peel them* under cold, running water.
> •*Rinse hands* frequently under cold water while chopping.
> •*Keep your* mouth tightly closed while chopping.
> •*Chop with* the exhaust fan operating.
> •*Or, wear* a diving mask.

Peas

• *Always cook* peas in the pod. The peas separate from the pods when cooked and the pods float to the surface. It's less work and the peas taste better.

Potatoes

• *Stick three* or four toothpicks into one of the long sides of the potato before placing it in a microwave oven. Stand it on the toothpicks, and it will cook more evenly.

• *Use the* water from boiled potatoes when making gravy.

• *And, use* the water from boiled potatoes instead of milk when mashing potatoes.

• *If you* peel more potatoes than you need, cover them with cold water and add a few drops of vinegar to the water. Refrigerate and they'll keep for several days. Be sure they're completely immersed.

Red cabbage

• *To keep* it from turning purple, add a tablespoon of vinegar to the cooking pot.

Sweet potatoes
• *For simple* peeling, take sweet potatoes from boiling water and plunge them immediately into cold water. The skins fall off.

Preventing boilovers
• *A toothpick* inserted between lid and pot before cooking will let just enough steam escape later to prevent messy boilovers.

Bugged out
• *To chase* insects from cabbage, cauliflower, and similar vegetables, soak the vegetables in cold water with a few tablespoons of either salt or vinegar for fifteen minutes.

FRUITFUL SUGGESTIONS

Ready to eat
• *These fruits* can be bought unripe and will ripen uncovered at home: avocados, bananas, honeydew melons, mangoes, papayas, persimmons.
• *Apricots, nectarines,* peaches, pears, and plums may be ripened at home in a loosely covered paper bag.
• *But these* don't get riper, so buy them ready to eat: apples, berries, grapes, grapefruit, pineapples, pomegranates, and rhubarb.

Apples
• *When baking* apples, remove a horizontal slice of peel from around the middle. Apples won't shrink while baking.

• *Soak cut* apple pieces in salted water for ten minutes. They'll remain crispy and won't turn brown.
• *Dried-out apples* will regain their flavor if you cut them up and sprinkle the pieces with apple cider.

Bananas

• *Ripen green* bananas more quickly by placing them near an overripe banana.
• *Or wrap* green bananas in a wet dish towel and put them in a paper sack.

Berries

• *Choose berries* with caps. If they're gone, the berries may be too ripe.
• *Wash strawberries* with caps on, *then* hull to preserve juices.
• *They'll last* longer if you store them unwashed and uncovered. Leave caps and stems on, too.

Dried fruits

• *To remove* the pits from dates, cut with a scissors dipped in water.
• *To chop* dates or figs, spray the chopping blade with nonstick cooking spray. Sticky fruits won't stick.
• *Eat fresh* figs at room temperature. Chilling tends to tone down the flavor.
• *For dried* out dates, raisins, and figs: steam them in a strainer over hot water.
• *Or place* them in a jar and sprinkle a little water over them; set in the refrigerator for a short time.
• *Or heat* in a 350° oven for a few minutes.
• *They'll stay* moist if you refrigerate them.

Grapefruit

• *Store it* in the refrigerator, covered with aluminum foil or waxed paper to prevent it drying out. Plastic rots it.

Juice
• *Store orange* juice made from frozen concentrate in a closed container or it will lose up to fifteen percent of its vitamin C per day.

Lemons
• *Submerging a* lemon in hot water for fifteen minutes before squeezing it will yield almost twice the amount of juice.
• *Or roll* a lemon on a hard surface, pressing with your hand.
• *If you* need only a few drops of juice, prick one end with a fork and squeeze the desired amount. Return the lemon to the refrigerator and it will be as good as new.

Melon
• *If the* stem is still attached or the scar is jagged, a melon was taken from the vine too early. If the cantaloupe is ripe, the stem scar will be smooth.

Oranges
• *If you* put oranges in a hot oven before peeling them, no white fibers will be left on them.

Peaches
• *Peaches ripen* quickly if you put them in a box covered with newspaper. Gases are sealed in.

Pineapple
• *When pineapple* isn't quite ripe, remove top and skin, slice and place in pot. Cover with water and add sugar to taste. Boil a few minutes, cool, and refrigerate. Fruit tastes fresh and crunchy.

EGGS-PERT-EASE

For the freshest eggs

• *Always buy* from a refrigerated case. At room temperature, an egg loses more quality in one day than it will during a week of refrigeration.

• *Store eggs* in their own carton, not in the refrigerator egg shelf, and they'll keep longer.

• *And if* you store eggs with the large ends up, they'll stay fresher.

Brown eggs vs. white

• *Brown eggs* are not more nutritious than white. The only difference is in the breed of chicken that lays it.

Beating egg whites

• *Use glass* or metal mixing bowls, not plastic. Plastic tends to retain grease, which can prevent whites from whipping up.

Warming eggs for beating

• *Eggs beat* to a greater volume when they're at room temperature, so try this if you don't have time to let eggs warm up naturally: put them in a bowl of warm water for a few minutes, then crack, and separate.

Finding fresher eggs

• *Buy brown* eggs one week, white the next. You won't wonder which eggs are the freshest when you alternate colors.

Eggs-cellent solutions for baking

• *If a* recipe calls for two whole eggs and the frosting calls for egg whites only, save on eggs by doing a little juggling. Use one whole egg plus two egg yolks in the cake and you'll have two egg whites left for the frosting.

Seeing through the shell
• *Add food* coloring to water before hard-boiling eggs. Then you can tell the boiled eggs from the raw ones in the refrigerator.
• *Or mark* hard-boiled eggs with a crayon or pencil before storing.

Yolklore
• *Keep yolks* centered in eggs by stirring the water while cooking hard-boiled eggs. Especially good for deviled eggs.
• *Keep yolk* intact when separating it from the white by breaking the eggshell and tipping the whole egg into the palm of your hand. The yolk will remain in your palm while the egg white runs between your fingers and into a small bowl.
• *Prevent crumbling* yolks by dipping your knife or egg slicer in cold water before slicing hard-boiled eggs.

All it's "cracked" up to be
• *You won't* drop the eggs if you moisten your fingers before removing them from the carton.
• *Rub a* cut lemon over eggshells to keep them from breaking while cooking.
• *Rescue an* egg that cracks while boiling by immediately pouring a generous quantity of salt on the crack. This tends to seal the crack and contain the egg white.
• *To peel* hard-boiled eggs easily, plunge them into cold water. Crack the shell, then roll the egg lightly between the palms of your hands and the shell will come right off.

Whites made right
• *Beaten egg* whites will be more stable if you add one teaspoon of cream of tartar to each batch of seven or eight egg whites.
• *Let egg* whites warm to room temperature before you beat them. Then, as you beat them, add slightly less than one tablespoon of water for each white to increase the volume.
• *Egg whites* will not beat satisfactorily if the least bit of yolk is present. Remove specks of yolk with a Q-tip or dampened cotton cloth to which they will stick. Also make sure the eggbeater is free of oil.

EASE WITH CHEESE

Hard facts
• *To keep* cheese from hardening, butter the cut end.
• *To soften* hardened cheese, soak it in buttermilk.
• *Store cheese* in a wine vinegar-soaked cloth for extra flavor and freshness.
• *To prevent* mold, store cheese in a tightly covered container with some sugar cubes.

Wrong is right
• *Cottage cheese* will remain fresher longer if you store the carton wrongside up in the refrigerator.

Cutting cheese straight
• *Keep your* eye on the part you're cutting from, not on the piece that's being cut off, and you'll cut it straight every time. This works for bread, too.

Prevent boxed cheese from sinking in the middle
• *Turn cheeses* like Brie and Camembert upside down to prevent sunken middles.

Grate hints
• *Brush a* little oil on the grater before you start grating and cheese will wash off the grater easily.
• *Force a* soft cheese through a colander with a potato masher instead of grating it.
• *Use a* potato peeler to cut cheese into strips for salads and other garnishings.

FEATS WITH MEATS

Bringing home the bacon
• *To keep* bacon slices from sticking together, roll the package into a tube shape and secure it with a rubber band before refrigerating.
• *Bacon curls* less if soaked a few minutes in cold water before it's fried.
• *For soft* but fully cooked bacon, keep a glass of water near the stove burner and dip each raw slice of bacon in the water before dropping it onto the skillet.

Sausage links and patties
• *Make sausage* broiling easy by pressing several links onto a meat skewer. One flip turns them all.
• *Prevent sausages* from breaking or shrinking by boiling them about eight minutes before they are fried.
• *Or roll* them lightly in flour before frying. This also gives them an appetizing, crunchy crust as they fry and helps prevent spattering.

Juicier burgers

• *Form patties* around chunks of cracked ice. When they're on the grill, the melting ice will prevent over-cooking.

• *For a* very moist burger, also put a few drops of cold water on both sides of the patty as you grill.

Faster burgers

• *Make lots* of hamburgers for a large crowd by cooking stacks. First, line baking pan with foil and arrange bottom tier of patties. Place another piece of foil over this layer and arrange the second tier. Stack them four deep. In a 350° oven the patties will be thoroughly done in about thirty-five minutes. Do the same for frankfurters, but cook for only fifteen minutes.

• *Or partially* cook the meat, using the above method, and finish off on the outdoor grill.

Mixing meat loaf

• *If you* don't like the mess of mixing meat loaf with your hands, use the dough hooks on your food processor or mixer.

• *Or, use* a pastry blender.

• *Or, wear* rubber gloves or plastic bags tied with rubber bands and work with your hands.

• *Or, place* all meat-loaf ingredients in a plastic bag, manipulate the bag and ingredients to mix and shape into a loaf, then slide loaf into pan.

Other methods for "loafers"

• *Meat loaf* won't crack while baking if you rub cold water across the top of the meat before you pop it into the oven.

• *Instant potato* flakes will bind and stretch your meat-loaf mixture.

When ham's too salty

• *After baking* it partially, drain all the juices, then pour a small bottle of ginger ale over it and bake until done.

Ham session

• *Have your* canned ham sliced by the butcher, then tie it back together, garnish with pineapple, and bake. No messy job of slicing it hot.

• *Ham will* be deliciously moist if you empty a bottle of cola into the baking pan and bake the ham wrapped in aluminum foil. Remove the foil about half an hour before the ham is done, allowing the drippings to combine with the cola for a tasty brown gravy.

Getting the rind off

• *Slit the* rind lengthwise on the underside before placing it in the roasting pan. As the ham bakes, the rind will pull away and can be removed easily without lifting the ham.

Roasts and steaks

• *Instead of* using a metal roasting rack, make a grid of carrot and celery sticks and place meat or poultry on it. The additional advantage: vegetables flavor the pan drippings.

• *For easier* slicing, let a roast stand for ten to fifteen minutes after removing it from the oven.

• *And when* broiling a steak, add a cup of water to the bottom portion of the pan before sliding it into the oven. The water helps absorb smoke and grease.

Tough meats

• *Tenderize tough* meat by rubbing all sides with a mixture of vinegar and olive oil. Let it stand two hours before cooking.

• *Or marinate* it in equal parts cooking vinegar and heated bouillon.
• *For a* very tough piece of meat, rub it well with baking soda, let it stand a few hours, then wash it thoroughly before cooking.
• *To stew* an old hen, soak it in vinegar for several hours before cooking. It will taste like a spring chicken.
• *To tenderize* boiled meat, add a tablespoon of vinegar to the cooking water.
• *When pounding* to tenderize meat, pound flour into it to prevent the juices from escaping.

ON TOP OF THINGS

Preventing skin on jellies, puddings, and sauces
• *Spread a* layer of melted butter or cream on top right after cooking. Stir and the skin and foam will disappear.

Gravy training
• *Keep a* jar with a mixture of equal parts of flour and cornstarch. Put three or four tablespoons of this mixture in another jar and add some water. Cover jar and shake it. In a few minutes you will have a nice smooth paste for gravy. Add mixture gradually to the pan, stirring the gravy constantly while bringing it to a boil.
• *For greaseless* gravy: Pour pan drippings into a tall glass. The grease will rise to the top in minutes. Remove it and prepare grease-free gravy.
• *Brown the* flour well before adding the liquid. This also helps prevent lumpy gravy.
• *A different* way of browning flour is to put some

flour into a custard cup and place it beside meat in the oven. When the meat is done, the flour will be brown, ready to make into a nice, rich gravy.

Instant white sauce

• *Blend together* one cup of soft butter and one cup of flour. Spread in an ice-cube tray, chill well, cut into sixteen cubes before storing in a plastic bag in the freezer For medium thick sauce, drop one cube into one cup of milk and heat slowly, stirring as it thickens.

BIRDS OF A FEATHER

No more fowl play

• *Defrost a* frozen chicken by soaking it in cold water that's been heavily salted. This draws out blood and the breast meat will be pure white.

• *An unpleasant* poultry odor can be neutralized if you wash the bird with the juice of half a lemon, then rub it with salt and lemon.

Time-saver

• *Debone chicken* with a pair of kitchen scissors. It is easier—much—than hacking and whacking with a knife.

• *Easy way* to cut an uncooked chicken is first to chill it thoroughly. How chilled? Just short of frozen is best.

Finger-lickin' chicken

• *To get* a light and delicate crust on coated, fried chicken: add about three quarters of a teaspoon of baking powder to the batter and use club soda as the dipping liquid.

Dumplings

• *Slice a* stack of flour tortillas into one-inch strips and add to a simmering stew ten minutes before the stew is done. This is cheap, easy, and good enough to fool dumpling experts.

• *To resist* the "sneak peak" temptation when making real dumplings, cover pot with a glass pie plate while dumplings are cooking.

Handle with care

• *Chicken will* be juicier if you use tongs to turn it during cooking. A fork will pierce the meat and let the juices run out.

The Thanksgiving thaw

• *Thaw the* turkey quickly in an ice chest or picnic cooler placed in the bathtub. Fill the cooler with cold water and change the water frequently.

Talking turkey

• *For a* juicier bird, fill a basting needle with one-quarter pound of melted margarine. Inject into raw turkey around breast and thigh in six to eight spots.

• *Unwaxed dental* floss is good for trussing because it does not burn and is very strong.

• *Or, instead* of sewing a stuffed turkey, close the cavity with two heels of dampened bread. Push each into an opening with crust facing out and overlapping to hold the stuffing in.

Instant unstuffing

• *Unstuffing a* turkey is a snap if you first tuck a cheesecloth bag into the turkey with the open edges hanging out. Spoon dressing into the bag until it's filled, then fold the bag closed. Tuck the edges up into the cavity. When the turkey's cooked, open the stuffing bag and spoon a little out. Then grasp the outside edges of the bag firmly and pull it out of the turkey.

Leftover turkey idea

• *Reheat on* top of the stove in a pan with about one-quarter cup of milk. Be sure to reheat over a low flame and turn the meat so both sides get heated evenly. Don't let the milk boil. The bird will taste fresh from the oven.

 WHEN THE DISH IS FISH

Take this bait

• *Thaw frozen* fish in milk. The milk draws out the frozen taste and provides a fresh-caught flavor.
• *Soak fish* in one-quarter cup of vinegar, wine, or lemon juice before cooking to make it sweet and tender.
• *Use a* piece of foil that's been crumpled and then smoothed out to bake fish sticks. Turn them over as required. They will brown evenly on bottom and top and won't stick, either.
• *Poached fish* will be firmer and whiter if you add a bit of lemon juice to the cooked liquid.

A GRAIN OF ADVICE

Different flavors for rice
• *Cook with* bouillon, vegetable, or meat broth instead of plain water.
• *Or, add* unsweetened pineapple juice for a tasty "pudding" treat.

No boilover
• *Cook long-grain* rice in a tea kettle with a removable lid. Spout keeps the rice from boiling over. The rice cooks faster, too.

Is it fresh
• *Whole-wheat flour* and brown rice will last up to a year in the fridge, only six months at room temperature.

USING YOUR NOODLE

Preventing boilovers
• *Lay a* large spoon or spatula across the top of the pot to reduce boilovers and splashing while cooking.
• *Or first* rub shortening around the top of the pot.
• *Or add* a pat of butter or a few teaspoons of cooking oil to the water. This also prevents pasta from sticking together.

Perfect pasta
• *Bring salted* water to a boil, stir in pasta, cover pot, and turn off heat. Let sit for fifteen minutes or until done.

• *When done,* run cooked spaghetti under hot—not cold—water before draining to prevent stickiness.

• *If you're* not going to serve spaghetti immediately, you may leave it in hot water if you add enough ice cubes or cold water to stop the cooking process. Reheat spaghetti by running it under hot tap water in the strainer while shaking it vigorously.

• *Use your* French-fry basket or a large strainer when cooking pasta. It's easy to lift the basket out of the water before rinsing the pasta and transferring it to the serving bowl.

Avoiding pasty pasta
• *Allow at* least five quarts of rapidly boiling water for one pound of pasta.

• *And add* a tablespoon of oil so the water doesn't boil over.

CONDIMENTS

Softening peanut butter
• *Add one* teaspoon of hot water. Stir.

• *Or,* drop in a little sesame oil. It not only restores creaminess, but increases the nutty flavor.

Homemade catsup
• *Combine one* cup of tomato sauce or mashed or canned tomatoes with two tablespoons of vinegar, one-quarter cup of brown sugar, one-quarter teaspoon of cinnamon and a dash each of allspice and ground cloves. A delicious change from bottled catsup.

The last of the catsup
• *Add a* few ingredients to bottle (or homemade) cat-

sup and make it into a tasty salad dressing. Add one tablespoon of vinegar, two tablespoons of oil and an eighth of a teaspoon or so of Italian seasoning to a nearly empty bottle of catsup. Shake well.

• *Or get* the last drops out of almost any catsup bottle, grab the bottom of the bottle and start swinging in a circular motion from your side. Just make sure you have the cap on tightly. The remaining drops will be forced to the top of the bottle.

Dressing up dressings

• *Improve bottled* blue cheese dressing with one-half finely chopped hard-cooked egg and one teaspoon of dry white wine to a half cup of dressing.

• *Freshen up* Green Goddess dressing with one tablespoon of chopped chives and a half to a full teaspoon of finely chopped parsley added to one-half cup of dressing.

• *Add flavor* and crunch to a half cup of Italian dressing with two tablespoons of chopped parsley, a half clove of finely chopped garlic, two tablespoons of grated carrots and a half teaspoon of lemon juice.

The "mayo" clinic

• *If your* cake recipe calls for oil and you've run out, you can substitute an equal amount of mayonnaise. You'll get a moist, delicious cake.

• *If you* rub the skin of a chicken with mayonnaise before baking, you'll get crisp, brown skin.

• *If you're* all out of oil when frying meat, use a few tablespoons of mayonnaise instead.

LET US SEASON TOGETHER

How much spice is enough
• *If a* recipe calls for fresh herbs and you've only got
the dried varieties, use one-third the amount of dried
herbs as a substitute. Drying concentrates flavors.

Rehydrating dried herbs
• *If you* don't like the crunchiness of dried herbs in
cold dips and sauces, try this: place the herbs in boiling water for thirty seconds, strain, pat dry, then use.

Bay leaves
• *Place bay* leaves in a tea ball for easy removal from
a stew before serving.
• *Or skewer* with a toothpick, making it easy to spot
them. The same applies for any other herbs, such as
garlic cloves, that don't dissolve as they cook.

Chives
• *To chop* chives a chopping board isn't necessary.
Take chives from the freezer and grate only enough
for use, returning the remainder to the freezer. Chives
taste just as they do when freshly chopped. This also
works with parsley.

Fresh herbs
• *Keep them* flavorful by shaking them in olive oil;
then refrigerate.
• *To release* flavorful oils from dried or fresh herbs,
rub them briskly between fingers.

Garlic
• *To get* the skins off garlic before chopping, pound
each clove with the side of a heavy knife, meat

pounder, or a bottle. The skin pops right off.
• *Or soak* garlic in warm water and the skin will peel off easily.
• *To make* fresh garlic salt: cut or mash garlic on a board sprinkled with salt. The salt absorbs the juices. It also reduces the garlic odor. And garlic won't stick to the knife if you chop it with a little salt.

Mint
• *Sprinkle a* pinch of sugar on mint when you chop it. Sugar draws out the juices and makes chopping lots easier.

Dry mustard
• *A half-teaspoon* added to a flour mix for frying chicken adds great flavor.

Pepper
• *A few* peppercorns in the pepper shaker will keep the holes from clogging while giving more of a fresh-ground pepper taste.

Onion salt
• *Make fresh* onion salt instantly. Cut a slice from the top of the onion, sprinkle salt on its juice, and scrape with a knife.

Rosemary
• *As rosemary* is a rather splintery spice, you may want to put it in a pepper grinder for grinding over foods.

Salt
• *A salt* shaker that delivers salt too fast can be easily remedied by plugging up some of the holes. Wash shaker to remove all salt, dry thoroughly, and use col-

orless fingernail polish to stop up the desired number
of holes.

• *Since most* recipes call for both salt and pepper,
keep a large shaker filled with a mixture of both. A
good combination is three-quarters salt and one-
quarter pepper.

A common error

• *Never keep* spices close to a kitchen range—they
lose their flavor and color. For best results, store in
refrigerator or any other cool, dry place.

IN YOUR CUPS

Filter tips

• *Paper towels* cut to size make inexpensive (or
emergency) filters for percolators or drip pots.

• *Remove some* of the acid taste of coffee by adding a
small pinch of salt before pouring in the boiling water.
Works for hot chocolate, too!

• *For clear* coffee, put unwashed egg shells in after
percolating coffee. Remember, always start with cold
water.

Your own mini coffee maker

• *Put a* teaspoon of drip coffee into a small strainer
(two and a half inches in diameter) and place in a cup.
Pour boiling water over grounds until cup is full. Let
steep to desired strength.

• *If you* wish, place mini coffee filters (make your
own) in the strainer before adding coffee.

Keeping tabs on your tea bag

• *Slip the* paper tab that's attached to the tea bag

under the cup before pouring water and the tab won't be pulled into the cup.

Tea-riffic flavorings
• *Add fragrance* and flavor to your tea by keeping a few pieces of dried orange rind in the canister.
• *Instead of* using sugar, dissolve old-fashioned lemon drops or hard mint candy in your tea. They melt quickly and keep the tea clean and brisk.
• *Add a* small amount of very hot water to instant tea before adding cold water. The crystals will dissolve completely for better flavor.

Did you know?
• *Dry table* wine will lose a good eighty-five percent of its calories and all its alcohol when stirred into cooked dishes. That means a 125-calorie glass of wine will only give you eleven calories in food. Pretty good—and so's the flavor.

Juice spruce-ups
• *Improve the* taste of an ordinary large can of tomato juice by pouring it into a glass bottle and adding one green onion and one stalk of celery cut into small pieces. After it stands for a while, it tastes like the more expensive, already seasoned juice.
• *Keep juice* cold without watering it down by putting a tightly closed plastic bag of ice into the pitcher.
• *Frozen orange* juice will have a fresh-squeezed flavor if you add the juice of two fresh oranges to the reconstituted frozen juice.

SAFETY MEASURES

• *Keep cold* water running in the sink while you pour hot water from a pot of vegetables. It prevents the steam from scalding your hands.

• *Don't let* oil heat to the smoking point. It may ignite. (It also makes food taste bitter and irritates your eyes.)

• *When broiling* meat, place a few pieces of dry bread in the broiler pan to soak up dripping fat. This not only eliminates smoking fat but also reduces the chance that the fat will catch fire.

JUST DESSERTS

Whip it up

• *Chill cream,* bowl, and beater well.

• *Set bowl* of cream into a bowl of ice while you're whipping.

• *Add the* white of an egg. Chill, then whip.

• *For stubborn* cream, gradually whip in three or four drops of lemon juice.

Neat work

• *To eliminate* a lot of mess when whipping cream with an electric beater, cut two small holes in the middle of waxed paper, then slip the stem of the beaters through the holes and attach the beaters to the machine. Place papers and beaters over the bowl and whip away.

• *Or do* the same thing using a paper plate.

Keep cream in shape

• *Preserve the* firm shape of whipped cream by using

powdered sugar instead of granulated sugar. The whipped cream won't get watery.

• *Cream that* is whipped ahead of time will not separate if you add a touch of unflavored gelatin (one-quarter teaspoon per cup of cream).

Oh! Fudge!

• *Fudge won't* sugar if you add a dash of cream of tartar.

Finding the capacity of a mold

• *When you* don't know how much liquified dessert you need to fill a decorative mold, fill it with water, then pour the water into a one-quart measuring cup. You've got your measurement now.

Good ideas for gelatin

• *Add two* tablespoons of cherry gelatin to an apple pie mix. Besides helping to thicken the pie, it will add color and flavor.

• *Add one* cup of plain yogurt instead of one cup of cold water to a gelatin dessert. You'll get a creamier, tarter flavor.

WHEN SOMETHING GOES WRONG...

Too salty

• *Add cut* raw potatoes to soup or stew, and discard them once they've cooked and absorbed the salt.

• *Or add* sugar.

• *Desalt anchovies* by soaking them in cool water for fifteen minutes. Remove and pat dry with a paper towel.

Too sweet
- *Add salt*.
- *Or add* a teaspoon of cider vinegar.

Too much garlic
- *Place parsley* flakes in a tea ball and set it in the stew or soup pot until it soaks up the excess garlic.

Brown sugar has gone hard
- *Grate the* amount called for with a hand grater.
- *Or soften* by placing a slice of soft bread in the package and closing it tightly. In a couple of hours the brown sugar will be soft again.
- *Or set* a cup of water alongside the brown sugar in a covered pan. Place in an oven on low for a while.

Butter isn't soft.
- *Grate it*.
- *Invert a* small heated pan over the butter dish for a while.

Food has burned
- *Remove the* pan from the stove immediately and set it in cold water for fifteen minutes to stop the cooking process. Then, with a wooden spoon, carefully remove the unburned food to another pan. Don't scrape, and don't include any pieces with burned spots unless they have been trimmed.
- *To remove* the burned flavor from rice, place a piece of fresh white bread, preferably the heel, on top of the rice and cover the pot. In minutes the bad taste should disappear.
- *Add a* teaspoon of peanut butter to gravy to cover up a burned flavor

Gelatin is sticking to the mold
- *Soak a* towel in hot water, wring it out, and wrap it

around the mold for about fifteen seconds. Then, with both hands, unmold with a quick downward snap of the wrists.

Gravy is
... too thin
• *Mix water* and flour or cornstarch into a smooth paste. Add gradually, stirring constantly, and bring to a boil.
• *Try instant* potato flakes instead of flour.

... too greasy
• *Add one* quarter teaspoon of baking soda to greasy gravy.

... too pale
• *Color with* a few drops of Kitchen Bouquet.
• *Or, mix* one tablespoon of sugar and one tablespoon of water and heat the mixture in a heavy pan until the water evaporates and the sugar starts to brown. Then pour the pale gravy into the sugared pan.
• *Or add* dark, percolated coffee to pale gravy. It will add color but won't affect the taste.

... not smooth
• *Put it* in the blender.
• *Use a* whisk.

Milk is scorched
• *Remove the* burned taste from scorched milk by putting the pan in cold water and adding a pinch (one-eighth teaspoon) of salt.
• *A small* amount of sugar added but not stirred will help prevent milk from scorching.
• *For easier* cleaning, always rinse a pan in cold water before scalding milk in it.

Pastries are charred
• *Cake: Let* it cook before scraping off the burned layer with a knife. Frost with a thin coating of very soft frosting to set crumbs. Then cover with another, thicker layer.
• *Biscuits: Use* a grater rather than a knife to scrape the bottom of burned biscuits. If you use a knife, you may end up holding a handful of crumbs.

Pasta is gluey
• *If drained* pasta is glued together, reboil it another minute or so.

Pastry dough clings
• *If it* sticks to the rolling pin, slip a child's sock (with the foot cut off) over it and sprinkle with flour.
• *Or place* the rolling pin in the freezer until chilled before flouring.

Vegetables are wilted
• *Pick off* the brown edges. Sprinkle with cool water, wrap in a towel, and refrigerate for an hour or so.
• *Perk up* soggy lettuce by adding lemon juice to a bowl of cold water and soak for an hour in the refrigerator.
• *Douse quickly* in hot water and then ice water with a little apple cider vinegar added.
• *Lettuce and* celery will crisp up fast if you place them in a pan of cold water and add a few raw sliced potatoes.

It's curdling
• *Mayonnaise: Start* over with another egg yolk and add the curdled mayonnaise drop by drop.
• *Hollandaise: Remove* sauce from heat and beat in

one teaspoon of hot water, a few drops at a time. Do not return to heat. Serve warm or at room temperature.
• *Or put* hollandaise in saucepan over hot water in a double boiler. Add sour cream by the teaspoonful until the sauce is smooth.

NOSE ENCOUNTERS OF THE WORST KIND

Banishing unpleasant cooking odors
• *While cooking* vegetables that give off unpleasant odors, simmer a small pan of vinegar on top of the stove.
• *Or add* vinegar to the cooking water.

Refrigerator and freezer odors
• *Place one* of the following "odor eaters" into a saucer and place it in your refrigerator: charcoal, dried coffee grounds, vanilla bean or extract on a piece of cotton, baking soda, or crumpled newspaper.

For odors that won't go away
• *When all* else fails, place a coffee can full of charcoal on the refrigerator shelf and leave it a few days. Repeat until odor is gone.
• *Make a* paste of baking soda and water and spread it all over the inside of the refrigerator. Use cotton swabs to ensure that you get every corner and crevice. Wait a few days before sponging off.
• *And make* sure the drain pan on the bottom of the refrigerator is clean.

Hand-ling a problem
• *To banish* onion, garlic, and bleach odors from

hands, put all five fingers on the handle of a stainless-steel spoon and run cold water over fingers.

Coverups

• *After cleaning* an oven, eliminate the lingering smell by baking orange peels in a 350° oven.
• *When the* trash compactor is running to full capacity, a few drops of oil of wintergreen will reduce odors.

7

Best of
Helpful Hints
for Family Business

FOR THE RECORD

Tracking down purchases
• *When enclosing* a check for a mail order purchase, write the company's name, address, and phone number on the check. The canceled check will be a complete record in case you want to reorder or replace a part.

Check this out
• *Do you* write checks before entering them in the ledger? You're less likely to forget to record them if you reverse the procedure and record them first.
• *Or, order* checks that come with a "carbonless copy" sheet attached; most banks now offer these. Keep the copies until you've entered the checks.

KEEPING IN TOUCH

Address file box
• *Instead of* updating address books, use a filing card system. In addition to addresses and phone numbers, you'll have room on the cards to keep track of children's names, birthdays, anniversaries, etc.

Phone numbers
• *Write emergency* phone numbers on a small card and tape it to the telephone. Cover the card with clear plastic tape. This can be a lifesaver.
• *And to* change addresses written in ink, use mailing-list labels (available in stationery stores).

Anniversary greeting
• *Make your* own greeting card in a flash by taking a snapshot of the family holding a sign saying "Happy Anniversary" or any other message.

This is a wrap
• *Before wrapping* a package for mailing, write the name and address on a slip of paper and place it inside the box. Should something happen to the address on the outside, the post office can get the address from the inside and send it along.

THE "WRITE" STUFF

When your pen slips
• *Correct spelling* mistakes in handwritten letters without completely rewriting them. Just place a piece

of typewriter correction tape over the errors and rub with a ballpoint pen. Most correction tape is white, but there are sheets you can buy in pastel colors that match stationery.

Cleaning ballpoints
• *If your* ballpoint becomes clogged with excessive ink and fuzz, insert it in the filter portion of a cigarette. Just a few quick turns and it's ready for use.

Renewing worn erasers
• *If pencil* erasers become too smooth to do their job, file with an emery board and they'll be like new.

Emergency pencil sharpener
• *Use a* potato peeler.

To find the starting end of the tape
• *For cellophane* or masking tape: tuck the cut end under about one-quarter of an inch. The tape makes its own little tab.
• *Or, attach* a penny to the end.
• *Or, place* a paper clip there.

ON THE BOOKS

A real page turner
• *If you* don't have a "rubber finger," just twist a rubber band around your index finger. But don't twist it too tight.
• *Or, use* the eraser on the end of your pencil.
• *Or, rub* a little toothpaste onto your fingertips and let dry.

Drying wet books
• *Dry the* pages and keep them from wrinkling by placing paper towels on both sides of every wet page. Close the book and let it sit overnight with a heavy book on top.

Dried spots
• *Non-greasy dried* spots can be removed from the pages if you rub them very gently with extra-fine sandpaper.

STAMP ACTS

Getting in your licks
• *When a* postage stamp won't stick, just rub it across the gummed part of an envelope that's been slightly moistened.

The problem is licked
• *Lick the* envelope where the stamp will be placed. You won't have to taste the glue and the stamp will stick on better.
• *Or, rinse* out an empty roll-on deodorant bottle, fill it with water, and keep it in the desk drawer.
• *Or, use* an empty, clean shoe-polish container the same way.
• *Or, simply* use a kitchen sponge.

Ungluing stuck stamps
• *Run a* warm iron over them, but separate the stamps quickly before the glue sets again.
• *Or, place* in a shallow dish or sink filled with water.

Let soak, then pull apart gently under slow running water. Dry them facedown on paper toweling.
• *Or, place* them in the freezer. They will usually come apart and the glue will still be usable.

EVERYTHING IN PLACE

House keys
• *The best* place to keep a spare set of house keys is with a trusted neighbor.
• *Or, bury* a set of keys nearby in a film canister.
• *To avoid* fumbling around for your house key, drill a second hole near the edge of the key so it will hang slightly off-center on your keyring.

How to preserve a favorite news clipping.
• *Dissolve a* milk of magnesia tablet in a quart of club soda overnight. Pour into a pan large enough to accommodate the flattened newspaper. Soak clipping for one hour, remove, and pat dry. Do not move until completely dry. Estimated life: two hundred years.

Get the picture
• *Store family* photos in a file box and use tab dividers to label them by year, event, or subject.
• *And put* the negatives in envelopes and keep them in the box right behind the prints.
• *Make slide* shows go smoothly as follows: first ensure that all the slides in the holder are inserted with the correct end up, then run a marking pen across the tops of the slides. Next time you need only look for the marks when putting slides in the holder.

Kids' stuff
• *Store the* youngsters' artwork, school papers, and other memorabilia in large boxes in their closets. Annually go through the boxes to discard the excess. Cover the boxes, label them, and store your memories in a safe place.

Family lost and found
• *A small* box in a convenient place may serve as a catchall for the little things found in odd places around the house.

Don't forget
• *When you* have an important task or appointment to remember, wear your watch on the other wrist. It will seem strange, and be a constant reminder to do what you're supposed to or get where you're going.
• *If you* tend to lose lists, write them out, then insert in a luggage tag with a see-through window. Hang the tag on your key chain.

The perfect spot
• *When finally* you find something after looking all over the house for it, put it back in the first place you looked. That's probably where it belongs.

IT'S YOUR MOVE

A picture is worth a thousand words
• *Planning to* sell your home in the fall or winter? Make sure you have pictures of its special summer features to show prospective buyers. Take a picture

of the apple tree and roses in full bloom, or of a family picnic under the shade tree.

• *Before moving* to a new house, take photos of your old house, your children's friends, the old school, and of anything else the family will have fun looking at later.

First things first

• *Set off* a bug bomb in the new house a day or so before moving in. Even the cleanest house sometimes has unseen bugs, and this will be your last chance before moving in the food, dishes, kids, and pets.

• *Have area* rugs and slipcovers cleaned before you move. They'll come back neatly rolled in paper, ready for moving. Or, if you're moving locally, the cleaner can deliver them to your new address.

• *If you're* moving to another state or city at some distance, be smart. Pack enough clothing for the first five days for everyone in the family. If the movers are late, you won't be caught without changes.

• *Make sure* the items you'll want first, such as beds, get packed in the moving van last.

• *And make* a box marked "special" filled with essentials such as bedding, light bulbs, a change of clothing, and other indispensables. Move it yourself so it doesn't get misplaced.

Get packing

• *Lawn and* leaf bags are great to pack blankets, clothes, and other soft items. They're less expensive than boxes and can be used to store items that are not needed right away.

• *Extra-large plastic* garbage cans are also great packing containers. Stuff them with unbreakables, or pack them with breakables that have been wrapped carefully in padding.

• *Use small* linens (towels, washcloths, pillowcases) as packing material for dishes. They protect dinnerware and don't take up extra space.

• *Stuff plastic* bags with crumpled newspaper and use them as buffers in packing cartons.

Bits and pieces

• *Collect all* casters, screws, and brackets in a plastic bag and tape them to the piece of furniture they came from.

• *Sectioned cardboard* boxes from liquor stores are great for packing glasses and other fragile items.

• *Press screws* and other hardware to a length of duct tape, then press the tape to the back or bottom of the item for which they're needed. Hardware won't get lost in transit. (But be careful where you apply the tape—duct tape can remove some finishes.)

• *When removing* pictures, attach the hooks to the back of each frame with masking tape.

Total recall

• *Take a* photograph of the arrangement of a complicated display of china and glassware in your cabinets. When you unpack in the new house, you'll have a handy guide for reassembly.

Moving the heavyweights

• *Put four* carpet tiles under the legs of heavy appliances when moving them. Turning the carpeting foam side up keeps the appliance from slipping off, and the carpet side slides easily over vinyl floors.

• *When there* just doesn't seem to be any place to grip a heavy piece of furniture, buckle several heavy leather belts together and slip them over an end or corner.

Tax deduction for moving
• *Remember that* moving expenses may be tax-deductible. Keep a file of bills of lading, packing certificates, travel expenses, and so forth.

MAXIMUM SECURITY

Open and shut cases
• *For extra* window security, drill holes through the frames where the upper and lower halves of windows come together. Put nails in the holes so they slip in and out easily. Insert them when you don't want windows to open and remove them when you do.
• *To prevent* a burglar from lifting a sliding door out of its track, put a two-inch corner brace on the inside top of the door.
• *Or, put* a length of wooden dowel or a broom handle on the track and the door can't slide open.
• *If you* have an attached garage, install a peephole viewer in the door connecting the house to the garage. That way, you can investigate a noise without opening the door.
• *Another way* to keep a prowler out of your garage is to put a C-clamp (ask for it at a hardware store) on the track in front of the roller. The garage door won't budge with the clamp in place.

Smoke detectors
• *When installing* smoke detectors, be sure to put one in the basement, too. A fire that starts here may not trigger the other alarms in your home until it's too late.

Under lock and key
• *Take photographs* of household valuables, furniture, and other items and keep them in your safe-deposit box. In case of fire or theft, you'll have evidence for your insurance claims.
• *And make* photocopies of your credit cards in case they are misplaced or stolen.

8

Best of
Helpful Hints
for Floor and Carpet Care

A CLEAN SWEEP

Collection agent
• *Dust and* dirt collect easier if you spray the bristles of the broom with some furniture polish or water.

Repellent action
• *Put a* coat of wax on your dustpan; dust and dirt will slide off easily.

Hard-to-reach places
• *Slip a* sock or two over the end of a yardstick and secure with a rubber band.
• *Or staple* a small sponge to the end of a yardstick to reach under the refrigerator and radiators.

TOPS FOR MOPS

Homemade floor cleaner
• *Combine one-half* cup of bleach, one-quarter cup of

washing soda, and one gallon of warm water. Great
for washing all floors except cork.

Cleaner mops

• *Rinse soiled* string or yarn mops in a bucket of
sudsy water and a little chlorine bleach as long as the
strings aren't coated with cellulose.

• *If your* string mop needs softening, dunk it in a fresh
pail of water to which you've added a capful of fabric
softener.

Do's for dust mops

• *Place a* nylon stocking over your dust mop. Discard
the stocking and you will have a clean mop.

• *Don't be* fazed if you can't shake a dust mop outside. Shake off dirt and dust after placing the mop
head inside a large grocery bag.

Mop to glow

• *Floors will* shine between waxings if mopped with a
mixture of one-half cup of fabric softener and one-half
pail of cold water.

• *Or, quick-shine* floors (after they have been swept
clean) with a mop and a piece of waxed paper underneath. The remaining dust will also stick to the waxed
paper.

Refresh a dull floor

• *If a* mopped floor dries with a film that dulls the
luster, pour one cup of white vinegar into a pail of
water and go over the floor again.

WAXING AND POLISHING

When you're out of floor wax
• *Add one-half* cup of vinegar and two tablespoons of furniture polish to a pail of warm water.
• *Or, add* a capful of baby oil to detergent and water.
• *Or, add* some skim milk to the wash water.

It's time to strip the old wax
• *Try this* solution: one cup of Tide laundry detergent, six ounces of ammonia, and one gallon of warm water.

Cleaning your floor polisher
• *If wax* has built up on the felt pads of your floor polisher, place the pads between several thicknesses of paper toweling and press with a warm iron. The towels will quickly absorb the old wax.

VACUUMING ADVICE

Two step savers
• *Make your* vacuuming easier by adding a thirty-foot heavy-duty extension cord to your sweeper cord.
• *Carry all* your attachments in a carpenter's apron.

Get the plug out
• *A straightened* wire coat hanger will unclog your unattached vacuum hose.

An old bag
• *Some vacuum* bags can be used many times. When

full, just cut off the bottom and empty it. Then fold and staple.

Cleaning under dressers
• *When you* must vacuum underneath it, take out the bottom drawers from a dresser that is too heavy to move. If the dresser does not have a wooden bottom, the vacuum hose will fit through the opening.

LOWDOWN ON LINOLEUM

Keeping it in place
• *A linoleum* floor tile may come loose or develop a bulge. Put a piece of aluminum foil over the tile and run a hot iron across the top a few times to soften the glue. Then put a couple of heavy books on the tile to flatten it.
• *The same* method can be used to remove floor tile.

Sticky issue
• *No linoleum* cement available and tiles won't stick to the floor? Apply a layer of denture cream to the back of the tiles. Put a few heavy books over the area and let dry for twenty-four hours.

Patch work
• *To patch* a hole or gouge in linoleum, grate a scrap of matching tile in a food grater, then mix the dust with white glue. Fill the hole with the mixture. Let it dry and sandpaper it smooth.
• *Or, make* a paste of finely chopped cork and shellac. Fill the hole, sandpaper it, and touch it up with paint to match the color of the linoleum.

To seal linoleum seams
• *Run a* strip of cellophane tape down the full length of the crack. Shellac over the tape and the surface will hold up indefinitely.

Touch-ups
• *Use automobile* touch-up paint to cover scratches and burns on linoleum. The paint won't wash off, even after many scrubbings.

Heel and crayon marks
• *Black heel* marks and crayon marks can be removed with a dab of toothpaste rubbed on with a damp cloth.

PROTECTIVE MEASURES

Easy glider
• *Glue pieces* of old carpeting to the bottom of chair legs. The chair will slide more easily and won't leave marks on the floor.

Eliminating marred floors
• *When moving* furniture, slip old heavy socks over their legs.

Rocking without worries
• *Your rocker* will not scratch waxed floors if you line the rocker arcs with adhesive tape.
• *Or, wax* the arcs of your rocker at the same time you do the floors.

WHEN THERE'S TROUBLE UNDERFOOT

Silence squeaks forever
• *Silence floor* squeaks by dusting talcum powder or dripping glue into the cracks.

A static and shock remover
• *Mix one* part fabric softener with five parts water in a spray bottle. Mist the carpet very lightly. Let dry and you'll have no more clinging pet hairs or unwanted carpet fuzz on clothing.

OUT OF THE CARPET BAG

Measuring for rugs
• *If you're* not sure how big a rug to buy, lay newspapers out on the floor to cover the amount of space you feel looks best. Measure, then find a rug to fit.

Longer carpet life
• *Don't use* leftover carpeting as an area rug on your new carpet unless it's backed with rubber. Because the bottom is rough, it acts like sandpaper, wearing down the pile whenever someone walks on it.

Carpet brighteners
• *One cup* of borax is an excellent carpet cleaner and deodorizer. Just sprinkle on and leave for one hour before vacuuming.
• *Or sprinkle* a generous amount of baking soda on the carpet before vacuuming.

Touch-ups
• *Bleached-out or* dingy carpet spots will disappear if you rub on permanent marking pens of the same color as the rug.

REPAIRING THE RUG

Are your throw rugs throwing you around?
• *If your* throw rugs are starting to slip and slide, apply some nonskid bathroom appliqués to the bottoms.
• *Or place* a few strips of double-faced carpet tape under the corners.
• *Or sew* or glue rubber jar rings on the bottom.
• *Or spray* on latex from a floor care supplier.

When the edges are frayed
• *To repair* a rug with frayed edges, snip off the loose threads and dab some transparent glue along the entire edge. When the glue dries, it won't be noticeable.

If your braided rug has split apart
• *Sew it* back together again with clear plastic fishing line.
• *Or, instead* of sewing, use clear fabric glue to repair. It's that fast and easy.

In case of a burn
• *Remove some* fuzz from the carpet, either by shaving or pulling out with tweezers. Roll into the shape of the burn. Apply a good cement glue to the backing of the rug and press the fuzz down into the burned spot.

Cover with a piece of cleaning tissue and place a heavy book on top. This will cause the glue to dry very slowly and you will get the best results.

Flattened carpet
• *If heavy* furniture has flattened the pile of your rugs, raise it with a steam iron. Build up good steam and hold your iron over the damaged spot. Do not touch the carpet with the iron. Brush briskly.

SPOT SOLUTIONS

Instant spot removers:
  • Prewash commercial sprays
  • Glass cleaner
  • Club soda
  • Shaving cream
  • Toothpaste

Apply one of the above to the stained area after checking for colorfastness in an inconspicuous area. Rub it in and wait a few minutes before sponging it off thoroughly. If the stain is still present, combine two tablespoons of detergent, four tablespoons of white distilled vinegar, and one quart of warm water. Work into stain and blot, blot, blot.

When the wine spills
• *Treat a* red-wine spill on the rug with ordinary shaving cream from an aerosol can. Then sponge off with cold water. Always test on an out-of-sight area first.
• *Or, immediately* cover the stain with a liberal amount of salt or baking soda. Leave until the stain is completely absorbed, then vacuum.

- *Or*, *remove* with club soda.
- *Or*, *remove* it with white wine.

Ballpoint ink marks
- *Saturate the* spot with hair spray. Allow to dry.
  Brush lightly with a solution of water and vinegar.

9

Best of Helpful Hints for Freezing

THE COLD FACTS

Rules of thumb

• *Don't refreeze* any thawed raw food. But cooked food, such as leftover turkey, that has been slightly thawed may be refrozen if it's still below forty degrees or if ice crystals are present.

• *If raw* food has thawed, you may cook it and then refreeze it.

• *Do not* refreeze ice cream (texture will change).

• *Do not* refreeze frozen juice (you lose vitamins).

• *Do not* refreeze anything creamed (because of possible contamination).

• *Freezing fruits* in juices enriched with vitamin C will help prevent browning.

• *Thaw food* in fridge, allowing six hours per pound.

On your mark...

• *If you* need a label in a hurry when freezing an item in aluminum foil, write food description on a plastic bandage, then peel off the backing and apply to foil.

126

Get set...

• *To freeze* food in plastic bags, remove as much air as possible. Gather the tip of the bag around an inserted straw, suck out the air, then remove the straw, and close the bag tightly.

• *Freezing expands* foods and liquids, so always allow at least one-half inch of space at the top of the container before putting it in the freezer.

• *Most foods* stick together when frozen, so flash-freeze them to eliminate this problem. Spread food on cookie sheet, freeze it, then remove, and wrap in air-tight container before returning food to the freezer.

• *Always steam* or scald vegetables before freezing as this prevents loss of color, texture, and flavor.

EVERYBODY FREEZE

Bacon

• *Lay strips* side by side on a piece of aluminum foil or waxed paper. Roll them up lengthwise so they don't touch each other and put the roll in the freezer in a plastic bag. The bacon can be cooked as soon as it is thawed out enough to unroll.

• *To freeze* bacon for a small portion, accordion-pleat some waxed paper and insert a strip of bacon in each fold. Wrap in freezer wrap and freeze.

• *Crumble those* extra pieces of cooked bacon and freeze them. Use as toppings for baked potato, in salad, or in scrambled eggs.

Blueberries

• *Freeze them* in the basket they come in, unwashed.

Wrap container in aluminum foil or plastic wrap. They will keep their color and shape.

Brown sugar
• *It won't* harden if stored in the freezer.

Bread (stale)
• *Cut into* tiny cubes. Brush with melted butter and toast them in the oven for later use as croutons. Then pop them into the freezer.

Butter
• *Save wrappings* from sticks of butter or margarine. Keep in the refrigerator in a plastic bag for future use in greasing baking utensils.
• *Unsalted butter* can be stored in the freezer indefinitely if it's wrapped and sealed airtight.
• *Salted butter* can be stored for a shorter period in its original container with no wrapping.

Cabbage
• *Wash and* dry a head of cabbage with paper towels, then wrap in a plastic bag, and freeze. When defrosted, the leaves are limp and easy to remove and handle. Perfect for stuffed cabbage—and you won't have the odor of boiled cabbage throughout the house.

Cheese
• *Parmesan and* Romano grate quite easily when frozen.
• *And fifteen* minutes in the freezer makes soft cheese easier to grate.
• *Keep packages* of blue or Roquefort cheese in the freezer. The cheese will crumble perfectly if scraped

with a paring knife and will be ready to serve with salad dressing by dinnertime.

• *Save the* tail ends of different kinds of processed, Swiss, feta, Cheddar cheese, then grate and freeze in an airtight bag. Top dishes that call for melted cheese like veal parmigiana, or use in omelets.

• *Cream cheese* dips can be frozen. If dip appears grainy after defrosting, whip it well.

Cookie dough

• *Pack homemade* refrigerator cookie dough into large juice cans and freeze. Thaw fifteen minutes, open the bottom, and push up. Use the edge as a cutting guide.

Cream

• *Leftover whipped* cream: Drop dollops of whipped cream on a cookie sheet, then flash-freeze before storing in plastic bags.

• *Pour a* can of evaporated milk into a freezer tray and freeze until ice crystals form. Whip it as you would heavy cream.

Eggs

• *Freeze whole* eggs in ice-cube trays that have been sprayed with vegetable oil. Freeze as many eggs as there are sections in the tray. Beat eggs gently in a bowl and add three-quarters teaspoon of sugar and one-quarter teaspoon of salt for every six eggs. Set a divider in the tray and pour the eggs into it. When eggs are frozen, place them in plastic bags. Each cube will equal one egg.

Fish

• *Here's how* to get your catch from your cabin back to town: use disposable aluminum foil loaf pans. Lay enough ready-to-cook fish for two servings in each pan, cover with water, and freeze. When solidly frozen, slip block out of pan, smooth the edges of the ice block, and then wrap in heavy-duty foil. Rinse loaf pans and reuse.

Ice cream
• *Sometimes ice* cream that has been opened and returned to the freezer forms a waxlike film on the top. To prevent this, press a piece of waxed paper against the surface of the remaining ice cream and reseal the carton.

Marshmallows
• *Flash-freeze—and* no more stale marshmallows!

Meat
• *The thicker* the meat, the longer it keeps in the freezer. It's less vulnerable to freezer burn and dehydration.
• *Alternate chopped* meat patties between waxed paper sandwich bags. This eliminates the job of separating them since the double thickness prevents sticking.
• *To defrost* frozen ground beef quickly, sprinkle it with the amount of salt you plan to use in cooking. Salt greatly speeds thawing.
• Maximum storage times (from USDA; at zero degrees):

fresh whole poultry, beef roasts, and steaks:	twelve months
lamb roasts, lamb chops, chicken parts:	nine months
pork and veal roast:	eight months
turkey pieces:	six months

                  pork chops, variety meats,
                  ground stew meats: four months
                  pork sausages: three months

Potato chips
• *When wrapped* and stored in the freezer, they don't
get soggy.

Sandwiches
• *Most sandwiches* can be stored in the freezer for
two weeks. Make them once every two weeks and
save yourself a lot of time.
• *Fillings that* can be frozen include cold cuts, peanut
butter (but jelly doesn't freeze well), cheese, meat
loaf and catsup, chicken, turkey, beef, and tuna-fish
salad. (Mayonnaise can be frozen if the filling is no
more than one-third of the sandwich volume).
• *To prevent* frostbite, wrap sandwiches very securely
in freezer paper or aluminum foil.
• *Pack sandwiches* for the lunch box right from the
freezer. They will thaw in time for lunch.

Soup stock
• *Pour it* into loaf pans, freeze, then remove from the
pans, and wrap in freezer paper. The blocks are easy
to store and take up a minimum of freezer space.

Tomatoes
• *Freeze leftovers* for use in soups and stews. They'll
be mushy, but that won't affect taste.
• *Put tomatoes* in the freezer unpeeled. They'll easily
slip out of their skins later.

10

Best of Helpful Hints for Furniture

GOOD-WOOD CARE

Polishing tools
- *A shoe* buffer polishes tabletops to a high luster.
- *A terry* cloth oven mitt does double duty. One side waxes, the other polishes.

The best dust cloths
- *Add two* teaspoons of turpentine to a quart jar of hot, sudsy water. Put clean, lint-free cloths in the jar and let them soak overnight, then wring them out, and hang to dry. Your cloths will attract dust as well as if they'd been sprayed with any commercial product.
- *Or, put* a cloth in a solution of one-quarter cup of lemon oil and two cups of hot water. Let the cloth dry, and go to work.
- *Capture dust* balls from under and behind furniture with a damp mop.

High-gloss shine
• *After polishing,* sprinkle on a little cornstarch and rub wood with a soft cloth. The cornstarch absorbs excess polish, eliminates fingerprints, and leaves a glossy surface. Your finger should leave no trace when you run it over the surface.

Polishing carved furniture
• *Dip an* old soft toothbrush into furniture polish and brush lightly.

ON THE SPOT

Cigarette burns
• *For small* minor burns, try rubbing mayonnaise into the burn. Let set for a while before wiping off with a soft cloth.

• *Burns can* be repaired with a wax stick (available in all colors at paint and hardware stores). Gently scrape away the charred finish. Heat a knife blade and melt the stick against the heated blade. Smooth over damaged area with your finger.

• *Or make* a paste of rottenstone (available at hardware stores) and salad oil. Rub into the burned spot only, following the grain of the wood. Wipe clean with a cloth that has been dampened in oil. Wipe dry and apply your favorite furniture polish. But always consider the value of the furniture. It might be worthwhile to have a professional make the repair.

To remove white water rings and spots
• *Remove white* water rings from furniture with a soft, damp cloth and a dab of white toothpaste, then polish as usual. Make sure you always rub along the grain of the wood.
• *For stubborn* stains, add baking soda to the toothpaste.
• *Make a* paste of butter or mayonnaise and cigarette ashes. Apply to spot and buff away with a slightly damp cloth. Polish as usual.

Removing candle wax from wooden finishes
• *Soften the* wax with a hair dryer. Remove wax with paper toweling and wash down with a solution of vinegar and water.

Removing glue from furniture
• *Airplane or* cement glue can be removed by rubbing with cold cream, peanut butter, or salad oil.

Removing paper that is stuck to a wood surface
• *Do not* scrape with a knife. Pour any salad oil, a few drops at a time, on the paper. Let set for a while and rub with a soft cloth. Repeat the procedure until the paper is completely gone.
• *Old decals* can be removed easily by painting them with several coats of white vinegar. Give the vinegar time to soak in, then gently scrape off.

Scratches
(NOTE: Make sure you always rub with the grain of the wood when repairing a scratch.)
• *Walnut: Remove* the meat from a fresh, unsalted

walnut or pecan nut. Break it in half and rub the scratch with the broken side of the nut.

• *Mahogany: Either* rub the scratch with a dark brown crayon or buff with brown paste wax.

• *Red Mahogany:* Apply ordinary iodine with a number 0 artist's brush.

• *Maple: Combine* equal amounts of iodine and denatured alcohol. Apply with a Q-tip, then dry, wax, and buff.

• *Ebony: Use* black shoe polish, black eyebrow pencil, or black crayon.

• *Teakwood: Rub* very gently with 0000 steel wool. Rub in equal amounts of linseed oil and turpentine.

• *Light finished* furniture: Scratches can be hidden by using tan shoe polish. However, use only on shiny finishes.

• *For all* minor scratches: Cover each scratch with a generous amount of white petroleum jelly. Allow it to remain on for twenty-four hours. Rub into wood. Remove excess and polish as usual.

• *For larger* scratches: Fill by rubbing with a wax stick (available in all colors at your hardware or paint store) or a crayon that matches the finish of the wood.

OUTSIDE HELP

Lawn furniture

• *Tubular aluminum* outdoor furniture won't pit if you apply paste wax. Repeat every year.

• *And keep* old metal furniture from rusting by drilling a few small holes in the seats. Rainwater will drain out.

• *To help* prevent moisture damage to cushions, first cover them with plastic, then put the covers on.

Outdoor furniture covers
• *Fold a* shower curtain in half and stitch up the sides to make pullover covers for collapsible outdoor furniture.

Wrought iron
• *If rust* appears, remove all traces with steel wool or a wire brush.
• *Coat with* aluminum paint before covering with two coats of outdoor paint.
• *A coat* of paste wax will give extra protection.

THE SHINING

Chrome furniture
• *Spiff up* chrome table legs by rubbing them with a piece of smooth, damp aluminum foil, shiny side out. The foil will turn black, but the chrome will sparkle.
• *Leftover club* soda is great for cleaning chrome. Ask your friendly bartender.

Glass-top tables
• *A capful* of liquid fabric softener in a quart of water makes a great lint-free cleaner for glass and Plexiglas tabletops.
• *Or rub* in a little lemon juice. Dry with paper towels and shine with newspaper for a sparkling table.
• *Toothpaste will* remove small scratches from glass.

Plastic tabletops
• *You will* find that a coat of Turtle Wax is a quick pick-up for dulled plastic tabletops and counters.
• *Or,* rub in toothpaste and buff.

SOFA, SO GOOD

Removing wax on fabric
• *Candle-wax drippings* on fabrics can be removed by placing a brown paper bag over the spot and running a hot iron over it. When the paper has soaked up some wax, discard it and use fresh paper. Repeat until the wax has disappeared.

Sectional furniture: keeping it all together
• *To keep* sectional pieces from drifting apart, fasten a small hook-and-eye set to the back legs.

Loose caster
• *Wrap a* rubber band or some string around the caster stem before pushing it back into the leg.

COVERING UP

Double-duty sofa
• *When it's* time to have the sofa upholstered, have one side of each cushion covered with plastic. When company comes, just flip the cushions over.

• *Because the* seat wears faster than the other parts, cover each seat cushion with two sets of covers.

Nonslip arms covers
• *Keep all* arm covers in place by laying a sheet of art foam (available in art-supply stores) between the arm covers and the armrest.

Having a fit?
• *Use a* rubber spatula to push the material into the corners and sides when fitting slipcovers.

Upholstery tricks
• *Space tacks* evenly on upholstered furniture by fastening a tape measure along the tack line.
• *When hammering* a decorative furniture tack, place a wooden thread spool against it to avoid damaging the head.
• *Stick a* few extra tacks to a hidden spot on the frame so they are available when needed.
• *After recovering* a piece of furniture, put some of the upholstery scraps in an envelope and staple it to the bottom of the piece. The material is there when a patch-up is needed.

Worn piping
• *When the* fabric wears off the piping on your sofa or chair, color it with matching indelible ink.

Removing blood stains from upholstery
• *Cover the* spot immediately with a paste of cornstarch and cold water. Rub lightly and place object in the sun to dry. The sun will draw the blood out into the cornstarch. Brush off. If the stain is not completely gone, try again.

Grease and oil stains
• *Sprinkle a* fresh stain with talcum, cornstarch, or fuller's earth. Rub in well until the stain is absorbed. Brush off and wipe with a damp cloth.

Soiled cotton upholstery
• *You may* have some success cleaning up small soiled areas with art-gum squares. You can purchase them at any stationery store.

Ready-to-use upholstery cleaner
• *Shaving cream* is one of the most useful upholstery cleaners for new stains and ordinary dirt.
• *Make your* own by mixing one half cup of mild detergent with two cups of boiling water. Cool until it forms into jelly, then whip with a hand beater for good stiff foam.

Vinyl upholstery
• *Never oil* vinyls because oil will make the vinyl hard. If this happens, it is almost impossible to soften it again. For proper cleaning, sprinkle baking soda or vinegar on a rough, damp cloth. Then wash with a very mild dishwashing soap. Body oil will cause vinyl to become hard, so it should be cleaned once in a while.

BE SEATED

Is your seat sagging?
• *Tighten a* drooping cane chair seat by giving it a hot

water bath and placing it outside in the sunlight to dry and shrink. After it has dried thoroughly, apply either lemon or cedar oil to prevent cracking and splitting.

• *Sagging springs* in chair: Turn the chair upside down. Make a pattern of the upper-structure frame. Transfer the pattern either to a piece of scrap masonite or plywood (⅛"). Nail to the upper structure. This will push springs back into the chair.

Wicker wisdom

• *To keep* wicker furniture from turning yellow, wash with a solution of warm salt water.

• *To prevent* drying out, apply lemon oil once in a while.

• *Never let* wicker freeze. This will cause cracking and splitting.

• *Wicker needs* moisture, so use a humidifier in the winter.

Rung master

• *Clean chair* rungs easily with a discarded cotton sock with spray wax on it.

ON THE HIDE

Proper cleaning and care for leather tabletops

• *Remove all* wax buildup with a vinegar and water solution (one-quarter cup of vinegar and one-half cup of water).

• *To raise* any indentations such as pressure points from lamps or ashtrays, apply lemon oil to the leather twice a day for a week. To maintain results, use lemon oil monthly.

Leather upholstery
- *Clean with* a damp cloth and saddle soap.
- *Prevent leather* from cracking by polishing regularly with a cream made of one part vinegar and two parts linseed oil.

11

Best of Helpful Hints for Garden and Plants

GOING TO POT

Repotting plants
- *Always choose* a pot that's not more than two inches larger in diameter than the old pot.
- *Blooming plants* should be repotted after they've blossomed, not before.
- *To help* reduce the shock of repotting plants, give the new soil a thorough watering.
- *Clay pots* should be soaked in water for a few minutes before you use. This prevents the clay from absorbing moisture from the potting soil.

Drainage for pots
- *Use pieces* of plastic screen instead of crockery shards to cover drainage hole. Repotting's a cinch, since roots grow right through the screen holes. And, a plastic screen doesn't rust.

Grouping small plants
- *Try a* wire rack that's used for holding glassware

and serving drinks. When it's time to water, take the whole rack to the sink. No need to remove the plants.

Tips for watering
• *A newspaper* or umbrella held behind the plant protects walls and furniture when spraying it.
• *Never put* clay pots directly on wooden furniture because water will seep through the porous clay.

Water ways for plants
• *An athlete's* water bottle (a plastic bottle with a bent straw) is great for watering hard-to-reach hanging plants.

Handy plant aids
• *Use a* meat baster for siphoning water runoff from large pots that are too big to move to the sink.

"Love 'em and leave 'em"
• *If you're* going away for a week, keep your plants healthy in a homemade miniature "greenhouse." First, thoroughly water the plant, then loosely wrap part of a plastic dry-cleaning bag over the plant and around the bottom of the plant.
• *If you* have many plants, fill the bathtub with about one-quarter inch of water. Set each plant on a saucer so that the pot doesn't touch the water and cover the whole tub with a dry-cleaning bag.
• *Another way* to keep houseplants watered while on vacation is to stand plants on bricks submerged in water in the tub. The bricks absorb water, keeping the plants happy.
• *Or, place* all houseplants in the bathtub on old thickly folded bath towels, in a few inches of water. They will absorb moisture as needed.

Ailing houseplants—"They'll reflect all the love you give them."
• *Your houseplant* will come out of a slump if you cover it with a plastic bag, along with a pest strip. Make sure the entire plant is under the bag. Remove the bag after a few days, and you will find the plant in good health. This is excellent to do when transferring plants into the house from the outside.

Cleaning plant leaves
• *Dust with* a feather duster
• *Glycerin is* one of the best substances to use if you wish to put a gloss on the leaves of your plants. Put a few drops of it on a cloth and swab the leaves with it. It is much better than olive oil or mayonnaise, since it is not a dust collector.
• *A half-and-half* mixture of milk and water also makes a fine solution for glossing leaves.

Bug beaters for houseplants
• *White flies:* Mix one teaspoon of dishwashing liquid in one gallon of water and spray on leaves.
• *Scales: For* instant removal of slugs, place plant in pot of water.
• *Pests of* all kinds: Plant a garlic clove along with your plant. As it grows, simply keep cutting it down so it will not disturb the appearance of the plant. Garlic will not harm the plant, but bugs hate it.

GRASS IS ALWAYS GREENER

The power is with you
• *A squirt* of an octane booster (available in auto-parts stores) will quickly start a stubborn lawn-mower motor.

• *To keep* screws from vibrating loose on power motors, apply some weather stripping sealer to the ends of screws. Screws will hold tight but are easily removed when necessary.
• *Unplug the* spark plug wire on the mower so youngsters can't start it while you're away.

Cutting up

• *Before cutting* tall, damp grass, spray the cutting blade of the lawn mower with vegetable oil spray, and wet grass won't stick.
• *Be sure* blades are sharp. Dull blades will rip rather than clip the grass and cause leaf tips to turn brown.

Carry along

• *Hang a* trash bag from the handle of the mower to fill with debris as you go.

Punch in

• *Wear golf* shoes when mowing on a wet or steep hill and aerate the lawn at the same time.

Patching bare spots

• *Use moss* to cover bare spots under trees (such as evergreens). Lay it on bare patches and water it well, and it should take hold.
• *If you* seed a bare spot on your lawn and don't have a roller, cover the patch with a wide board and walk on it.

NUISANCE CONTROL

No need to weed

• *Why clip* the grass that grows along walls by hand?

Make a mowing strip around fences and walls to eliminate hand-trimming chores. Strips can be made from
stones or bricks placed even with the soil.
• *Or dig* a shallow trench and fill it with a mixture of
sand and used motor oil or strips of plastic covered
with dirt.
• *If you* find that weeds are still growing between
your mulch or gravel, try this: lay plastic over the
area and place the mulch on top.

Good-bye to unwanted grass and weeds
• *Salted boiling* water will immediately kill grass or
weeds growing between sections of cement walk.
• *And use* salt sprinkled on the area to keep grass
from growing between bricks in a walk.

Clearing away poison ivy
• *Spray the* area with a solution of two gallons of
soapy water and three pounds of salt. A few dousings
will kill it.

Dandelion exterminator
• *Don't let* dandelion seeds blow all over your yard:
Hook a vacuum cleaner up to a grounded long exten-
sion cord and vacuum the seed heads.

WATER WAYS

The right way to water
• *A little* water is worse than none at all, when it
comes to watering your lawn. Don't even start the job
unless the ground is going to be drenched, and the soil
wet at least an inch below the surface. Reason? Light

watering causes the roots of grass to turn up and become shallow. A thorough watering once a week does a lot of good, whereas light watering every day or every few days does a lot of harm.

Soaking wet

• *If the* soaker hose is longer than the stretch of lawn that needs watering, shut off the extra portion of hose with a clamp-type pants hanger.

• *If the* soaker hose will not lie flat on the lawn, tape pieces of a yardstick to the bottom side.

• *A coat* hanger can be fashioned into a good support for a hand-held hose.

New tricks for old hoses

• *Punch a* few more holes in it and turn it into a lawn soaker.

• *Cut short* pieces of hose, slit them, and slip them on to insulate a lug wrench and a jack handle so your hands won't freeze when using these tools during the winter.

• *Slit sections* and attach them to the edges of your youngsters' swing seats. The hose acts as a bumper if the swing accidentally hits one of the kids.

Nozzle Keeper

• *Fasten a* broom clip or pound a nail above the outside faucet. Whenever you take the nozzle off the hose, just hang it and it won't get lost.

Easier toting

• *Keep your* garden hose coiled in a bushel basket. It'll be easier to carry around. You can store the hose in it, too.

FERTILE IDEAS

Read the label
• *Be smart:* Buy fertilizer on the basis of nitrogen content rather than price per bag. Inexpensive fertilizer may have a low nitrogen content. High nitrogen is better for your garden.

A matter of leverage
• *Use a* broom or snow shovel to move a heavy sack of fertilizer.

Spreading the benefits around
• *Distribute additional* fertilizer under trees so the grass can compete with the trees for nutrients.

For easier distribution
• *Make your* own fertilizer spreader from a large coffee can by punching lots of holes in the bottom. Cover with the plastic lid and shake the can.

Feeding time
• *There is* nothing better than compost to feed a garden. It can't be bought. It can only be made. Grind leftover vegetables, onion skins, and eggshells in a blender, then sprinkle compost around the garden. Use coffee grounds, too.
• *Large plastic* ice-cream containers make fine storage bins for collecting compost in the kitchen.
• *Pile leaves* and grass clippings in a corner and cover them (to prevent scattering). As the leaves decompose, they create a rich mulch for your garden.

TOOLING AROUND

Half a bottle
• *Here's a* handy tool carrier! Cut off the top of an old bleach bottle above the handle.
• *Or, cut* it off below the handle—use it as a scoop for pesticides and fertilizer.

Golf cart gardening
• *You'll be* using it on a different kind of green, but it works: Stash shovel, rake, and pitchfork in the bag and gloves and smaller tools in the bag's pockets. Wheel the cart around with you as you work.

Marked to measure
• *Inches marked* off on your garden trowel with red nail polish conveniently show proper depth for planting seeds and bulbs.

Easy handl-ing
• *Paint the* handles of all your garden tools in the same bright color so you can easily see them. If anyone borrows a tool, the color will be a reminder to return it to you.

Storage tip
• *Tools won't* rust if you leave them in a box of sand mixed with old motor oil.

BEATING AROUND THE BUSHES

Hold that line
• *To make* sure your hedges are trimmed in a straight line, tie a string to a branch at one end and run it across to the other end. Stand back to make sure the string is straight before you start cutting.

Prudent pruning
• *Keep your* pruning shears sharp, as dull blades leave ragged cuts that may not heal.
• *Protect your* hands while pruning. Use barbecue tongs or pliers to hold thorny branches.

Catch-all
• *Put a* sheet of plastic beneath the shrubs when clipping. Pick up the plastic for easy disposal of the trimmings.

Kid stuff
• *Use a* toy rake to reach those difficult spots underneath bushes and shrubbery.

Tree don'ts
• *Don't plant* trees too close to the house, or they may cause damage to the foundation.
• *Don't plant* them near a garden where they will block out sunlight and soak up nutrients.
• *Don't dig* the planting hole without laying a sheet of plastic next to it. When you're ready to fill the hole, just lift the edge of the sheet and the dirt will slide right back in.
• *Don't plant* a tree in soil that has poor drainage. Check by filling the hole with water. If it hasn't drained in twelve hours . . . think twice.

GONE TO SEED

An old-seed test
• *How do* you tell whether old seeds are still good? Count out about fifty seeds, placing them between two layers of wet newspaper covered with a plate. After five days, count the number of seeds that have germinated, to determine how thickly they will have to be spread. If half are no longer good, use twice as many as you normally would.

Off to a fast start
• *Place seed* trays on top of the refrigerator. Extra warmth radiating from the fridge helps seeds germinate.
• *Or, place* the trays of seeds in plastic bags, tie shut, and put on top of a console TV set.
• *Or, when* starting seeds in a window box, lay cotton balls on the soil. They retain moisture when you water. Remove the cotton when seeds start sprouting.

Soaking seeds
• *If some* seeds need to be soaked before planting, drop them in a wide-mouthed Thermos with warm water. Strain the seeds when they're ready.

Mixing seeds with talcum powder
• *If your* seeds are gathered in a clump, talcum powder will separate them so you can get better distribution while sowing.

Covering seeds with soil
• *Old, large* paintbrushes are great for covering seeds you've just planted in a row. Brushes give you more control and help you cover seed with just a few swipes.

Protecting seedlings with plastic straws
• *Cut the* straws into one-and-one-half-inch pieces, then slit each piece lengthwise. Slip a section around a stem before transplanting. Straws will keep cutworms from destroying plants.

Rootings
• *Use small* glass spice bottle for rootings. The plastic pouring lids keep stems separate and delicate roots can be seen at a glance.
• *When rooting* any plants in a glass of water, place aluminum foil around the top of the glass, then poke holes in the foil. Insert the cuttings. Rootings will stay tangle-free and separate, and the water won't evaporate as quickly.

Miniature greenhouses to make yourself
• *Cut bottoms* off plastic gallon milk jugs and stand tops over very young plants. Make sure to leave caps off for ventilation. Keep jugs in place until plants outgrow them.

HOW DOES YOUR GARDEN GROW?

Identifying plants
• *Make your* own markers from foam meat trays. Cut trays into triangles, write the plant's name in indelible ink on the wide end, and push the pointed end into the soil.
• *Or use* spring-type clothespins that have the name of the plant, number of seeds, and the date printed on them. Clip to the pot.

Plotting and planting
• *Make even,* parallel rows for planting with a child's toy wagon. Have one of your kids sit in the wagon for added weight as you pull. If the kids aren't around, use bricks.

Fertilizing with ashes
• *Once in* a while, sprinkle wood ashes evenly over the soil. Ashes are about fifty to seventy-five percent lime, and help control pH levels in soil.

On your knees
• *Make a* waterproof knee pad for gardening from an old pillow wrapped in plastic.

Portable chairs
• *Prefer to* sit while you weed? Nail a small board to an old paint can. Instant portable seat.

Scarecrows
• *Here's one* to make yourself: cut a plastic trash bag into long strips and staple them to the lip of a paper cup. Glue or nail the cup to a five-foot stake and set it out in your garden. When the plastic strips blow in the wind, birds will stay away.
• *Or, if* you want to safeguard a larger area, string up a clothesline to cross the garden and knot the plastic strips along the line.
• *Or, place* pinwheels in strategic spots. Kids love them but birds don't.

You'll get a boot out of this
• *If you'll* be working in a muddy garden and you're planning to (or have to) keep running in and out of the house, try this: set two grocery bags at the door, step

into them from the garden, go into the house without tracking dirt, then step out of the bags when returning to the garden.

Hauling leaves
• *Use an* old plastic wading pool.

BEING SUPPORTIVE

Attaching a trellis
• *Fasten it* with a hinge at the bottom and a hook-and-eye latch at the top so it can easily be pulled away from the house when you want to paint it.

Do-it-yourself trellis
• *Check with* companies that install chain link fences for odd-shaped discards that they might be willing to give away or sell cheaply. Narrow pieces are great support for climbing plants, and they look good, too.
• *Or, make* a trellis with five wire hangers. First make a stake from a two-by-four cut to four feet long. Using U-shaped staples, staple the hangers to the stake, so the hook on each hanger overlaps the preceding one.

 ## BOUQUETS FOR YOU

Frog substitute
• *The plastic* baskets that strawberries come in, turned upside down, make great holders for cut flowers in low, round bowls.

When the vase is the wrong size
• *If it's* too tall, crinkle a plastic bag and tie it loosely with a rubber band, then stuff it into the bottom.
• *Or, use* marbles.
• *If the* bouquet is small, stand a well-washed olive jar inside the vase. Filled with water and flower stems, the jar won't show in either opaque or crystal vases.
• *When flowers* are too short for any vase, make a centerpiece by floating a plastic doily in a bowl of water, then poking the stems through the holes.

Rose float
• *Keep those* roses that may have snapped off their stems. Just clip the stem completely off and float the rose in a shallow clear glass bowl filled with water and a quarter teaspoon of sugar.

Spring is bustin' out all over
• *In winter* when flowers are scarce, go out and prune some twigs or branches of forsythia, crab apple, hawthorn, lilac, and other flowering trees and shrubs. Put the stems in a bucket of warm water, then drop in a cotton ball saturated with ammonia. Put the pail and branches in a plastic bag and tie securely. Soon the ammonia fumes will force blooms on the branches.

Flower buds
• *If you're* buying flowers to decorate for a party, you can buy them two days in advance if the buds are closed. They'll open just in time.
• *Or, hurry* them open by adding warm water to the vase.

Ways to help your cut flowers last longer

• *Aspirin tablets,* pennies, and ice cubes are all said to lengthen the lives of fresh-cut flowers. However, the best preservative is actually two tablespoons of white vinegar and two tablespoons of cane sugar in a quart of water. The vinegar inhibits the growth of organisms and the sugar serves as food.

• *Drop a* penny into the vase, so tulips will stand erect and not open too wide.

• *Put a* piece of charcoal in the water and cut flowers won't develop a bad odor when the stems begin to rot.

Saving money on flowers

• *If you* group two or three narrow-necked vases together, you'll get a dramatic arrangement with only six flowers.

• *You might* save some money by stopping at the florist late at night. Sometimes you can get large quantities of unsold blooms at a discount. But remember, they aren't the freshest. If the guests for whom you're decorating stay past the cocktail hour, they aren't the only ones that might start drooping on the vine.

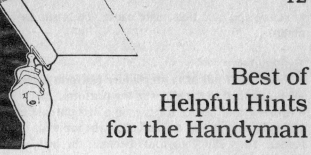

12

Best of
Helpful Hints
for the Handyman

BEFORE YOU BEGIN

A "hefty" apron
• *Make a* quick apron for those messy jobs by cutting holes for your arms and head in a large garbage bag.

Keeping track of small parts
• *Before taking* apart an item that has a lot of small pieces, stick a strip of double-sided tape on your worktable. Place the parts on the tape in the order of removal. Everything will be in line for reassembly.

LADDER MATTERS

In the can
• *Drive spikes* through the bottom of tuna-fish cans into the ground and put the feet of the ladder inside the cans.
• *And for* extra safety, wrap a piece of burlap around the bottom rung. Wipe your shoes on it to remove

moisture and mud that might cause you to slip as you climb.

Tool holder
• *Tools won't* fall off a stepladder platform if mould-ing is attached to the edges of the platform.
• *Make a* tool holder for use on a straight ladder by wrapping and nailing an old belt to the top ends of the ladder. Then slip your tools beneath the belt before you put the ladder up.
• *Or use* thick rubber strips from an old inner tube.

KNOTTY MATTERS

Straightening wire
• *Remove the* kinks and bends by passing it in and out of the tines of a fork, pulling it to straighten.
• *Or, holding* tightly to one end, pull as you press with a cold iron.

Preventing nylon cord and rope from fraying
• *Shellac the* ends of the rope and it will not unravel.
• *To prevent* nylon cord or twine from fraying at a cut end, heat the end over a small flame. The strands will bond into a solid unit. Knots can be prevented from working loose by this same method.

STICKY PROBLEMS

Shovel dilemma
• *To prevent* snow from sticking to a shovel, cover shovel with spray wax.

Nonslip bookends
• *Keep bookends* from slipping out of place by placing a sponge-type fabric softener under each bookend.
• *Or, cut* a rubber stair tread to fit the bottom of the bookend and glue in place.
• *Or, use* double-sided tape.

Make Con-Tact paper easy to work with
• *Store it* in the freezer first and the paper will be easier to handle and cut.
• *If your* Con-Tact starts to bubble, cut a small *X* in the bubble with a razor blade. Then carefully smooth the *X* into place.
• *If you're* applying paper in drawers and on shelves, use a blackboard eraser to make creases and bubbles disappear in a jiffy.

FOR THE SAND MAN

Sanding small items
• *It's lots* easier to sand small items if you tack sandpaper to a flat surface, then rub the object over it rather than holding the object and trying to sand it. Saves fingers.

Sanding places hard to get at
• *Cut a* piece of sandpaper to fit an ice-cream stick and glue it on.
• *Or, use* an emery board.

After sanding a surface
• *Pull an* old nylon stocking over your hand and rub

lightly over the wood. You will be able to locate the slightest rough spot.

Repairing bulletin boards
• *This is* great for a light-colored cork bulletin board that has become worn with age. First sand lightly with very fine sandpaper, then spray it with clear furniture polish. Good as new!

Refinishing cedar closets
• *If your* cedar closet no longer smells like one, lightly sand its surfaces. Sanding opens the wood's pores and restores cedar odor.

Longer-lasting sandpaper and easier sanding
• *Sandpaper will* last longer, work better, and resist cracking if the paper backing is dampened slightly, then wrapped around a block of wood.

PICTURE PERFECT

Preventing experimental holes when hanging pictures
• *Cut a* paper pattern of each picture or mirror that you plan to hang and pin it to the wall. After you've found the correct positions for the hangers, perforate the paper with a sharp pencil to mark the wall.
• *Before you* drive nails into the wall, mark the spot with an *X* of cellophane tape. This trick will keep plaster from cracking when you start hanging.
• *When the* landlady says, "No nails in the wall," hang pictures with sewing machine needles. They hold up to thirty pounds.

• *A wet* fingerprint shows the exact spot for the hanger. The print dries without a mark (if your hands were clean!).

For hanging pictures

• *Fishing line* is as strong as twisted wire. But if it shows above the top of the frame, it's nearly invisible.
• *If a* picture tilts despite everything you've done, try gluing a piece of wide rubber band to each lower corner on the back of the frame.
• *Or, stick* a blob of florist's clay on the back of the frame and press firmly against the wall.

Preventing frame from marring walls

• *Push rubber* headed nails into the lower corners. Buy these nails in the plumbing section of the hardware store.

FURNISHING A SOLUTION

Squeaky bedsprings

• *A shot* of spray wax will often silence the squeak.
• *If springs* rubbing against the frame cause the squeak, pad the frame with small pieces of sponge.

Wobbly table

• *If your* table wobbles because of a short leg, put a small amount of Plastic Wood on waxed paper. Set the short leg on it and allow to dry. Trim down with a sharp knife and smooth with sandpaper.

To loosen joints

• *Put vinegar* in a small oil can and apply liberally to joints, to loosen old glue.

Slipcovering a sponge rubber cushion
• *The cushion* usually sticks to the fabric, right? It won't if you do this. Cut a large plastic bag open along both sides. Slip the closed end of the bag over the end of the cushion. The slipcover should slide easily over the plastic bag. To remove the bag, just push one side of it down under the cushion, and pull it out on the other side.

Cutting foam rubber
• *This can* be one of the most frustrating jobs, but here's how to make it simple. Measure and draw a line on the foam rubber, put a board along the line, rest your weight on it, and cut along the line with a sharp knife dipped in water.

WHAT A PANE

Blocking the view
• *For temporary* bathroom privacy, frost the window by brushing on a mixture of four tablespoons of Epsom salts and a half-pint of stale beer.
• *Or, block* the view but let in light by using aquarium paint from a hobby shop.

Broken glass?
• *To pick* up shards of broken glass, mop the area with a piece of soft bread or damp paper toweling.

SHOW THEM THE DOOR

End marred walls
• *Keep doorknobs* from hitting and scuffing your walls by placing a small thumbtack on the spot where the knob hits.
• *Or, stick* a small adhesive-backed felt pad to the center of the knob.

Keeping cupboard doors shut
• *If cupboard* doors keep flying open, clip a few pieces of magnetic tape and stick them on the inside of doors at the frame. They'll work like a magnetic catch.

Emergency doorstop
• *Use a* tablespoon turned upside down with the handle pushed under the opened door. Works best on carpeted floors.

Hang it right
• *Hanging a* door will be a lot easier if you rest it on a small stack of newspapers or magazines while you put the hinges on the frame.
• *Remove a* door by taking off the bottom hinge first. Then wedge a book under the door and remove the top hinge.

HAMMER AND NAIL

Eliminating hammer and plier marks
• *When pulling* a nail out of wood with a claw ham-

mer, slip a small piece of wood or a magazine under the hammer-head. This protects the wood surface— and gets better leverage.
• *Or*, *use* a spatula or a bowl scraper.
• *To prevent* vise jaws from leaving clamp marks, pad them with plastic coffee-can lids.
• *Or*, *use* a kitchen sponge or carpet scraps.
• *For pliers*, cut two fingers off an old pair of rubber gloves and slip them over the jaws.

Starting nails ouchlessly
• *Hold the* nail between your fingers palm up—keeps knuckles out of the way.
• *Or*, *slip* it between the teeth of a comb.
• *Or*, *hold* it upright with a bobby pin.
• *Or*, *make* a notch in a cardboard scrap and position the nail in the *V* while you hammer.

 NOT-SO-SCREWY IDEAS

Difficulty loosening a tight screw
• *Put a* few drops of peroxide on the tight screw and soak for a few minutes.
• *Or soak* it with ammonia.
• *Or soak* it with penetrating oil.
• *If those* fail, try this: heat the nut or screw with an iron and rap it with a hammer. Use workman's goggles (get them at a hardware store) for eye protection.

Loosening a rusted bolt
• *You can* often loosen a rusted bolt by applying a cloth soaked in any carbonated beverage.
• *A drop* or two of ammonia will loosen it right up.

• *Before screwing* it back in, wrap thread around it and coat with Vaseline to prevent future rusting.

Screwing it in
• *A screw* will be easier to insert if you push it into a bar of soap first.
• *Keep a* bolt tight simply by putting another nut on the bolt and tightening it against the first one.
• *Or, put* a few drops of clear nail polish on the bolt just before giving it the final turn with a screwdriver.
• *Paint the* screw of a wobbly drawer knob with fingernail polish before inserting it. When the polish dries, it will hold the screw tightly.
• *Or, dip* screw in glue or putty and it will hold tight.

No magnetic screwdriver?
• *Start a* screw in a hard-to-get-at place by keeping it on the screwdriver while you work: push it through a narrow piece of masking tape, sticky side up, then fold each end of the tape so that it sticks to the sides of the screwdriver blade.

Is your screw loose?
• *Remove the* screw. Stick a wooden kitchen match in the screw hole and break it off. Replace screw and tighten.
• *Or, wind* a few strands of steel wool around the threads of the screw before screwing it in.
• *Or saturate* a cotton ball with Elmer's glue. Gently push the entire cotton ball into the hole. Allow it to dry at least twenty-four hours, then insert the screw gently with a screwdriver.

Aid for appliances
• *Should metal* screws on your home appliances keep coming loose, a dab of shellac placed under the heads

before tightening them will hold them securely in place.

CURES FOR CRACK-UPS

Mending a leaking vase
• *Coat the* inside with a thick layer of paraffin and allow it to harden. The paraffin will last indefinitely and the vase will not leak.
• *Or use* crayon that matches. Here's how: hold a match under the pointed end of the crayon and drip wax into the crack. Scrape away excess wax when it's cooled.

Mending a cracked cup
• *A simple* way to remove cracks in china cups is to simmer the cup in milk for thirty to forty-five minutes, depending on the size of the crack. If the crack is not too wide, the protein in the milk will seal it.

WHAT'S IN STORE

Storing small parts
• *Separate nails,* screws, bolts, and other small items and put them into baby-food jars with screw-on tops. Then punch a hole in the center of each lid, screw it in place under a work shelf, and screw the jar to the lid.
• *Keep nuts* and washers together by slipping them over the open end of an extra-large safety pin. Close the pin and hang it on a nail.

Storing larger tools

• *Hang a* shoe bag with pockets above your workbench.

• *Store your* circular saw blades in record-album covers and line them up in a record rack. Label the covers clearly and keep rack where children can't get at it.

Storing often-used tools

• *The tools* used most frequently should be stored in an old lunch box. The box is ready at hand in case of an emergency.

Storing seldom-used tools

• *Before storing* seldom-used tools, spray them with silicone lubricant, then wrap each tool tightly in aluminum foil.

Preventing rust on tools

• *Place a* piece of charcoal, chalk, or several mothballs in your toolbox to absorb any moisture.

• *Or,* wax tools with an automobile paste wax. A light coat will ward off corrosion for quite some time.

• *Or,* store small tools in a bucket of sand.

Keep this hint on file

• *Clean a* file by putting a piece of masking tape over the length of the blade and press down firmly. Pull the tape off and the shavings will come off with it.

Sanding disk holder

• *Cut a* paper plate in half, stack, then tack the halves to the shop wall for convenient storage.

Storing saw blades

• *Slit a* piece of garden hose and insert the teeth into it.

HERE'S TO GLUE

Gluing clamps for small objects
• *Use a* spring-type clothespin to hold a glued object in place as it dries.
• *Or,* use a clamp-type pants hanger.
• *And for* a very small item try an old screw-type earring.

A gluing clamp for larger objects
• *Wrap them* in masking tape until the glue dries. It's as good as a metal clamp.

Gluing joints
• *When gluing* a joint, put a strip of tape along the edge. If any of the glue is forced out of the joint, it will stick to the tape. When the job is done, just peel the tape off and any excess glue will come off with it.
• *For a* stronger bond, mix a few steel-wool shavings in the glue before applying.

Cap it off
• *If you* lose the cap from a glue bottle after the tip's been cut off, you can still keep the glue from drying out. Just put the cap from a ballpoint pen on the open tip.

Glue substitute
• *Try clear* nail polish for small repairs.

First aid when gluing chairs
• *When gluing* together a wooden chair or stool that has cross-pieces between the legs, the problem is keeping tension on all the parts. Use the tourniquet technique: after gluing, tie a strip of old sheet around

the whole thing, insert a small piece of wood under sheet, and twist the piece of wood until the sheet is holding as tightly as desired. Then secure the piece of wood by tying it to the strip of sheet.

TOP DRAWER

Easy drawer pull
• *If a* drawer's lost its pull, open it with a suction cup or plumber's rubber plunger.

Sticky dresser drawers
• *They will* slide easily again if you rub candle wax or soap on the runner of the side that seems to be sticking.

WHERE'S THE LEAK?

Finding a gas leak
• *Lather the* pipes with soapy water. The escaping gas will cause the soapy water to bubble, revealing the damaged areas. You can make a temporary plug by moistening a cake of soap and pressing it over the spot. When the soap hardens, it will effectively close (and mark) the leak until the gas man comes.

Leaking the blues
• *Checking for* a silent leak in the toilet-tank valve? Pour some bluing into the tank. Don't flush for an hour or more. Then, if blue water appears in the bowl,

seepage has occurred and either you or your plumber
should replace the valve.

PLUMB PERFECT

Taking the plunge
• *Putting a* towel or cloth in the overflow opening
when you're using a plumber's helper in sink or tub
will improve the suction.
• *Put some* petroleum jelly around the rim of your
plunger to provide a seal for better suction.
• *If your* toilet is clogged and you don't have a
plunger, try pouring six to eight buckets of very hot
water into the bowl as fast as they will go down without overflowing. Do not flush between buckets.

When the weather outside is frightful
• *Thaw a* frozen water pipe with a hair dryer.

Unclogging the drain
• *Pour in* a cup of salt and a cup of baking soda, followed by a kettle of boiling water. If the problem is
grease, it will usually dissolve immediately and open
the drain.
• *Or put* a heat lamp or hair blow dryer (turned to
hot) directly under the sink trap until the grease has
melted. Flush the drain by running hot water for a few
minutes.
• *You can* also run your garden hose into the house
and push the nozzle as far into the drain as possible.
After wrapping a towel around the hose to fully close
the drain opening, hold on tightly while someone else
turns on the outdoor faucet. Whatever is clogged
should be forced out by the water pressure.

APPLIANCE REPAIR

Shake, rattle, and roll
• *If your* stereo rattles, take the speaker apart and you'll probably find a crack in the paper cone. A dab of clear nail polish will mend it well.

Repeat performances
• *Your appliance* or car refuses to make its peculiar noise for the serviceman? Then tape-record one of its better performances and let him listen.

Letter perfect
• *Renew the* worn dial on a washer or other appliance by rubbing the knob with red or black crayon until indentations (letters and numbers) are level. Wipe off excess crayon and the print will be readable again.

WOOD-N'T YOU KNOW

Lumber hints
• *To prevent* moisture damage, stack your shop lumber on top of a couple of old tires.
• *Your shop* floor becomes a giant ruler for measuring lumber if you paint inch and feet intervals on it. Start at a wall so that wall and boards can abut.

Working with dowels
• *Heat wooden* dowels first in a medium-warm oven to get all the moisture out before using them. When you do use them, the wood will reabsorb moisture from the air and expand, making a much tighter joint.

OIL'S WELL

Slick oil tricks
• *Put a* drinking straw over your oilcan spout when oiling hard-to-get-at places.
• *Or, after* soaking the tip of a pipe cleaner, bend it to fit into any hard-to-reach spot.

SEEING THE LIGHT

Light bulbs
• *To remove* a broken light bulb, turn off the power, then press a thick, dry sponge onto the jagged bulb base and twist gently.
• *Or, use* a bar of soap.

Finding the right switch in a fuse box
• *You want* to turn off the power to a certain room, but you don't know which switch to flip. Try this: plug in a portable radio in that room, turning it up loud enough to hear at the fuse box. When you flip the right switch, the radio will shut off.

Power failure
• *Paint the* flashlight handle with luminous paint. It'll be easier to locate in the dark, in an emergency.
• *And, if* you're using candles during a power outage, put the candle and holder in a large, shallow dish filled with water. Water reflects the light and makes things a bit brighter—plus, you're lessening possible fire danger from a tipped-over candle.

To store a long extension cord
• *Straighten out* a wire coat hanger, keeping the hook at one end. Bend the hanger up toward the hook to form a large loop on which to wind the cord. Then hang the unit in a closet.
• *Or simply* wind the cord loosely and slip it into a cardboard tube (from paper towels or toilet paper).

Saving energy with outdoor switches
• *A dab* of bright nail polish applied to the "on" position can show you whether a light's still burning even in daylight.

Finding your keys
• *Attach a* piece of fluorescent tape to both sides of your house key and car keys. In the dark, you'll still be able to fish them from your purse or pocket.
• *If you're* constantly locking yourself out, start carrying two keys: one on a ring, another in your change purse.

GET SHARP

Razor blades
• *Don't cut* yourself when working with a double-edged razor blade. Make a holder by sliding a piece of cork over one edge.
• *Or, cover* one edge with the bottom fold on any empty matchbook. When you're done, close the cover, mark it "razor blade," and store it in a safe place.
• *To sharpen* blades, use the matchbook striker.

Whetstone flowerpot
• *Sharpen a* knife on the rim of a clay flowerpot to razor sharpness. Sharpen by keeping the blade of the knife almost flat on the rim.

13

Best of
Helpful Hints for
Holidays and Entertaining

IT'S YOUR PARTY

Invitations with flair

• *Write the* invitation on blown-up balloons with felt markers. Let them dry, then deflate. Then mail them to guests, who must blow up the balloon to read the invitation. (Great for a kids' party.)

• *Cut a* picture of a celebrity or funny situation from a newspaper or magazine, paste on plain paper and write an appropriate message, followed by party details: time, place, date. Photocopy and mail.

• *Hand-print invitations* to a more formal party on a plain folding paper fan. Tie a thin silver ribbon around it and mail in a business-size envelope.

• *For a* party with a sports theme: Make colored-paper pennants and write all the details on them in white ink. Cut the points off toothpicks and glue to the wide end of the pennant. Mail in a matching color envelope.

• *Or, send* beer coaster invitations. Give all information on the blank side.

A catered affair
• *Check to* see if your caterer charges by the plate.
Guests having seconds and thirds at a buffet may actually drive your total cost higher than a sit-down din-
ner would.

PARTY PIZZAZ

It's a housewarming
• *If you're* expecting guests who have never been to
your new home, put a colored light bulb in your yard
or porch and tell them to look for it.

For the bride
• *It's fun* to have each guest bring a favorite recipe,
along with a utensil used for preparing the dish. For
example, a Chinese recipe with a wok, an omelet recipe with an omelet pan, a meat-loaf recipe with a loaf
pan. The hostess could provide the bride-to-be with a
recipe box to store all her new recipes.

Keep things moving
• *For a* livelier party it's always best to have more
guests than seating. This will keep your guests min-
gling, rather than sitting down.
• *And, for* the same purpose, try to set out the food at
some distance from the beverages.
• *If your* apartment is small, the guest list large, and
you only want to prepare for a party once, try this:
stagger the hours you ask guests over for. The first
fifteen to twenty invitations can be for 5 to 7 P.M., the
next ten or so for 6:30 to 8 P.M., and the last list of

people for 7:30 to 10 P.M. There'll be just enough overlapping of friends without too much of a crunch.
• *Or you* can have a party in the evening and brunch the next morning. Get double use of flowers, rented chairs, etc., and plan the menu to double up on ingredients: Leftover ham goes into a quiche, fruit becomes fruit salad.

HIGH SPIRITS

Keeping the fizz
• *Bring out* the champagne. But if you don't drink it all, here's a way to keep it bubbly for a week longer. Drop a stainless-steel turkey skewer into the bottle and fasten a balloon over the neck with a rubber band. This will trap the carbonation.

Recorking the bottle
• *Lost the* cork to a wine bottle? Soften a candle stub, wrap it in paper toweling and insert it into the neck of the bottle.
• *Wine from* jugs that have been opened can be rebottled and its life extended by being poured into smaller bottles. But be sure to leave very little air space between wine and cork.

Here's a corker
• *To remove* the cork from the inside of a beautiful empty wine bottle, pour some ammonia into the bottle and set in a well-ventilated spot. The cork will disintegrate in a few days.

Punch for a bunch
• *It's easy* to serve hot punch in a thirty-cup coffee

maker. Remove the basket and there's plenty of room for ice.

• *Or use* a crockpot to control temperature. What could be easier?

Out of ginger ale?
• *Mix equal* parts of Coke and 7-Up. You won't be able to tell the difference.

A bowl with punch
• *Mix a* wine punch in advance so ingredients blend better. To serve the punch fresh and bubbly, add well-chilled club soda just before serving.

• *Fill a* crystal punch bowl with cold tap water an hour or so before using it. Chilling protects crystal from cracking later when ice is added.

• *Melting cubes* won't affect your punch if you use cubes made by freezing a moderate amount of punch in ice-cube trays.

• *Or make* punch "cubes" by filling small rubber balloons and freezing them. Wash balloons thoroughly first, of course.

• *For huge* cubes to keep punch cold, fill washed milk cartons or salad molds with water and freeze them. When ice is partially frozen, add fruit for a colorful touch. The larger the cube, of course, the more slowly it melts.

Swizzlers with sizzle
• *Use cucumber* sticks as swizzle sticks in Bloody Marys.
• *Use candy* canes for eggnog drinks.

Using your noggin with leftover nog
• *Pour nonalcoholic* eggnog into ice-cube trays. When almost frozen, insert wooden sticks to create

"eggnog-sicles" for you or the kids.
• *Or,* thaw frozen eggnog to use as a dessert topping for ice cream, cake, or fruit. Great, even after the holiday season's over.

ICE CAPADES

In the bag
• *Make your* ice cubes in advance. After they're frozen, store them in brown paper bags and they won't stick together.

For crystal-clear cubes
• *Boil water* first, then chill in refrigerator and freeze.

Keep it on ice
• *Fill a* large bowl with crushed ice and place a bowl of potato, shrimp, or fruit salad in the ice up to the rim. Add a little kosher or ice-cream salt to make it colder.
• *To keep* a salad, dip, or beverage really chilled, first weight your salad bowl down inside a large bowl filled with water and freeze. Then remove from freezer and fill empty center bowl. Your dish will keep its cool throughout the meal. Note: Use only temperature-resistant bowls in the freezer.

Preventing meltdown
• *Keep ice* from melting by putting dry ice underneath a container of regular ice.

Cube display
• *Freeze red* and green maraschino cherries in ice

cubes. Or cocktail onions, mint leaves, or green
olives for martinis on the rocks.

Tray chic

• *Ice cube* trays won't stick to the freezer compartment when a rubber fruit-jar ring or waxed paper is
placed under the tray.

• *Ice cubes* won't stick to metal trays as much if the
trays are seasoned as you would a new frying pan.
Coat them with oil, wait a day, then wash with mild
soap and warm water.

CREATING A MOOD

Faking baking

• *Before guests* arrive, give your home that "What's
bakin'?" fragrance. Sprinkle cinnamon and sugar in a
tin pie pan and burn it slowly on the stove.

Laying the cloth

• *Don't forget* to spray your prized linen tablecloth
with either spray starch or fabric protector. Spills will
be easier to remove.

Candle righting

• *Thin candles* won't stand up? Twist a rubber band
around the base before inserting it into the holder.

• *Or, keep* candles firmly in place with a little florist's
clay in the holder.

• *Is your* candle too large for the holder? Trim the
excess with a hot, sharp knife.

• *Large, round* candles can split and crumble when
pressed onto the spike of a holder. Avoid this by making a hole in the bottom of the candle with a hot nail.

Slow burns
• *Candles burn* more slowly and evenly with minimal dripping if you place them in the refrigerator for several hours before using.
• *Make candles* drip-proof by soaking them in salt water (two tablespoons of salt per candle and just enough water to submerge).

Hot tip
• *To light* candles in tall, deep containers, use a lit uncooked piece of spaghetti.

Candlestick makers
• *Clay flowerpot* saucers make great, inexpensive candle holders.
• *Or,* use a demitasse saucer.
• *Or, cover* small blocks of wood with Con-Tact paper or wallpaper, then drive small nails through the bottoms to hold candles in place.

Brighten and lighten
• *When candles* become dull and lose their newness, spray furniture polish on a cloth and wipe them thoroughly. They'll look new again.
• *Or, wipe* with rubbing alcohol.

SERVING SUGGESTIONS

Nature's own cups
• *Use a* large green pepper as a cup for dips. Cut off top, scrape pepper clean of ribs and seeds, then fill with sour cream or other dip.

• *Slice cucumber* in half lengthwise, scoop out seeds, salt, and drain. Then fill.
• *Use halved* and hollowed-out melon or orange as a cup to fill with cut fruit.
• *Serve beef* stew in a whole cooked pumpkin. Seed and rinse pumpkin with milk. Bake at 350° for forty-five minutes to an hour, until tender but not too soft. Ladle in the warm stew.

Jumbo bowl
• *Salad for* a crowd can be served from a vegetable crisper that you've removed from the fridge.

An extra serving dish
• *Your ice* bucket is insulated, so it will keep foods either hot or cold.

Serve without spillovers
• *To prevent* dishes and tumblers from sliding on a serving tray, place them on damp napkins.
• *Or, for* silver trays, use a sheet of plastic wrap.

It's fun to flambé
• *Any dessert* wine can be used to flambé. First, heat the wine over a low flame until it starts to boil. Reserving a tablespoonful, pour the rest of the heated wine over the food. Then carefully ignite the tablespoon of hot wine and pour over the food to flambé it. If the original liquor in a flambé pan refuses to light, heat fresh liquor in a spoon, pour over food, and ignite.

HERE COMES PETER COTTONTAIL

The best way to dye Easter eggs
• *Eggs should* be hard-boiled and chilled before dyeing for best results.

Great toss-away dye containers
• *Use clean* cans. Start saving the ones from soups and vegetables a few weeks before egg-coloring time.

Easter egg hunt
• *If your* kids won't eat hard-boiled eggs, organize a hunt for egg-shaped containers from panty hose filled with Easter "grass," jelly beans, and other goodies. Start saving them now.

PUMPKIN TIME

Halloween sandwiches
• *Cut out* a jack-o'-lantern's face on a slice of very dark pumpernickel bread. Place a few slices of cheese on a second piece of bread and top with the "carved" piece. Toast the sandwich lightly under the broiler and you have pumpkin sandwiches.

Keeping pumpkins firm
• *To preserve* Halloween pumpkins, just spray the inside and outside surfaces with a spray-on antiseptic to kill bacteria and keep the pumpkin in shape.

Miniature jack-o'-lanterns
• *Draw pumpkin* faces with a black permanent mark-

ing pen on some oranges. Stand them in a row on the
fireplace mantel or windows for a cute, inexpensive
decoration.

The safest, best-lit jack-o'-lantern yet
• *Cut a* hole in the bottom of the pumpkin just deep
enough to hold a miniature flashlight. Carve the
pumpkin as usual and flip on the light. It's lots safer
than candles.

HAVE A HEART

A Valentine cake
• *Make a* heart for your Valentine: first bake both a
round and a square cake. Cut round cake in half, then
turn the square cake so the corners face you in a diamond shape. Place each half of the round cake on the
two uppermost sides of the diamond. Now you have a
perfect heart-shaped cake. Frost and serve.

WRAPPING IT UP

Packing cookies
• *Keep those* plastic baskets from berries. Line each
with a paper napkin and fill with Christmas cookies or
candies.
• *Use long* plastic tomato trays. Line one with a
doily, set up cookies in it, then top with a second tray.
Seal with cellophane tape and wrap.
• *Cover a* coffee can with holiday paper, fill with

candy, cookies, or puzzle pieces and trinkets. Top with its plastic lid, then wrap.

Presents to be mailed
• *Stuff plastic* dry-cleaner bags with crumpled newspaper. Use as buffers when packing and newsprint won't rub off on the wrapping paper.
• *Protect the* bow from being crushed by covering it with a plastic berry basket (like the ones strawberries come in).

For easy paper cutting
• *Pull apart* a table with leaves, lay the paper over the slit, and cut with a sharp knife or a single-edge razor.

Homemade gift wrap
• *Make your* own inexpensive paper with white tissue paper and food coloring. Layer three or four sheets of tissue and fold them in half, in half again, and in half again. Now dip the corners only into solutions of food coloring—one color per corner. Be sure you don't soak the paper. Let the tissue dry out on newspaper, unfold, then iron flat.

Making used wrapping paper and ribbon new again
• *Wrinkled paper* perks back to life! Lightly spritz the wrong side with a little spray starch, then press it with a warm iron.
• *Run wrinkled* ribbon through a curling iron.

Cut to ribbons
• *Make your* own ribbon by cutting almost any type of fabric into the desired width and length. Striped material is perfect to cut in even widths. Press between sheets of waxed paper with a hot iron. The wax

keeps the strip from unraveling and provides enough stiffness for the ribbon to hold its shape when made into a bow.

• *Or use* paper that matches or contrasts with your gift wrap and cut long strips about a half-inch wide. Curl with scissors and glue down to the box top. If you don't want to use the paper right off the roll, use scraps.

A handy string dispenser

• *Make a* hole in the center of a L'Eggs panty-hose container lid and thread the string through the hole.

It is better to give . . .

• *For wrapping* an extra-large gift, try a Christmas tablecloth made of paper. It's easy to handle and less expensive than several sheets of wrapping paper.

Storing wrapping paper

• *Simplify the* storage of gift wrapping by placing rolls of it in a tall, narrow wastebasket. Tape a bag to the side to hold tape, scissors, pen, and tags.

Floral tribute

• *Don't toss* out that bouquet of plastic flowers you're tired of. Clip the stems and use the flowers to trim gift boxes.

GIFT RAPPING

Great expectations

• *For the* father-to-be: give a waiting-room kit. Fill a box with change for the telephone, telephone numbers of close relatives and friends, cigars, gum, lighter, his favorite magazine, and whatever else you can think of to keep him busy.

Unexpected bonus
• *When a* friend requests a special recipe, you can turn it into a special occasion by giving one of the expensive ingredients along with the copy of the recipe: a bottle of wine for beef Burgundy, wild rice for a favorite casserole, or shrimp for a dip.

A last-minute gift
• *Keep a* bestselling cookbook or two available and quickly add an inscription.

Show it's loved
• *When your* children receive a gift, take a picture of them playing with it or wearing it and send it as a thank-you note.

CHRISTMAS...ALL THROUGH THE HOUSE

Dish this out
• *Sift a* little cornstarch over hard Christmas candy when you put it in the dish. Stir. Candy will not stick together or to the dish.

Fruitcake refresher
• *To restore* a dried-out fruitcake, turn it upside down, poke a few holes, and drop in some frozen orange juice. The juice will melt slowly and spread through the cake instead of running right through. After the juice has melted, turn the cake over and the holes won't show.

• *Keep fruitcakes* fresh indefinitely by wrapping them in a damp towel.
• *Dampen the* towel with wine for a special flavor.

Card keeping
• *If there's* a special card you want to keep, give it a coating of hair spray. That prevents colors from fading.

Before spraying artificial snow on windows
• *Spray lightly* with nonstick cooking oil. The snow will wipe right off when the holiday's over.

Setting up
• *When assembling* an artificial tree, dip the ends of the branches in petroleum jelly before inserting into the frame.
• *To remove* tree-pitch from your hands, rub them with salad oil and wipe with a paper towel.

Decorating the tree
• *When different* strings of tree lights are all tangled together, try this: plug in one set and, by following the lights, untangle one string at a time.
• *Use green* pipe cleaners to tie tree lights to the branches.
• *Stiffen crocheted* Christmas ornaments with a few shots of hair spray.
• *A few* small bells hung low on the tree will announce that little fingers or paws are busy there.
• *Put "icicles"* in the freezer for a few days before using. They'll be static-free.
• *The baby* may have outgrown her crib mobile, but it's got another life: Just detach the figures from the main post and hang them on the tree.

To catch the overflow of gifts
• *Open a* colorful, man-sized umbrella and fill with presents. Tie red ribbon bows around the tip of each rib and a big bow on the handle. (This is a good place to keep gifts for guests who'll drop in over the holidays.)

Substitute clips for outdoor lights
• *Fasten lights* with spring-type clothespins.
• *Or, use* wrapped wire ties.

Taking the tree down
• *To prevent* tangled tree lights, store them around empty gift-wrap tubes. Push the plug into the tube, then wrap the lights around the outside and secure the end with a rubber band. Several strings of lights can be stored on the same tube.

Leftover wrap
• *For a* New Year's table centerpiece, draw a large round clock face. Surround it with noisemakers and confetti and curled paper made from leftover Christmas wrap.

14

Best of
Helpful Hints
for Your Health

For best and safest results, we recommend following these hints with care. For any medical issue—for example, starting an exercise program—check with your doctor first.

NUTRITION FACTS AND MYTHS

Did you know...
• *The best* time to take vitamins is after a meal, not before. It's the interaction with food in your stomach that makes them effective.

Are your vitamins potent?
• *Vitamins can* lose up to half their strength if they're old or improperly stored.
• *Your vitamins* are likely to be fresher if you buy them from a busy store where the turnover is frequent.

• *Check the* expiration date on vitamins and avoid those that do not have it in print.
• *Buy in* small quantities.
• *At home,* store the vitamins out of sunlight and away from moisture. If you keep them tightly capped, in a cool dry closet, they'll keep for up to two years.

B vitamins—natural pep-up

• *Brewer's yeast* is the best source of all the B vitamins except B-12 (which is generally added to it). Disguise the icky taste by adding it to orange juice.
• *Both coffee* and tea destroy vitamin B-1.
• *Lightly toasted* bread retains more of the B vitamins than dark toast.

The gassiest foods

• *Along with* baked beans, they include: milk, milk products, onions, celery, carrots, raisins, bananas, apricots, prune juice, pretzels, bagels, wheat germ, and brussels sprouts.
• *Most people* will find beans less gas-producing if they've been soaked in water for several hours. Though soaking removes some nutrients, it also removes most of the indigestible sugars. Before cooking beans, discard the water they've been soaking in and replace with fresh water.
• *Or, add* a tablespoon of baking soda.
• *Or, put* washed beans in a pot with four to five inches of water, stir in salt to taste and one teaspoon ground ginger per pound of beans. Soak as usual, then cook. Ginger won't change the taste of beans but is very effective in reducing gas.

Savvy cook

• *Air breaks* down some nutrients, so boil water

briefly before adding food. The boiling will force the air to escape.

• *Don't add* baking soda to green vegetables to improve their color. It destroys vitamins.

• *Scrub vegetables* and cook with their skins on. The fiber in the skins keeps the nutrients in during cooking.

If the label doesn't tell you enough

• *If you* need additional nutritional information about a product—number of calories, amount of salt, etc.—write to the company's consumer affairs division. The address should be on the label.

WINNERS FOR LOSERS: DIET TIPS

Sweet versus sour

• *Some tastes* clash with each other. Knowing this, perhaps you can make an urge go away. If you want a sweet, chew a lemon. Or drink a glass of diet soda if you yearn for something salty.

Keep it simple

• *Don't plan* elaborate diet menus. Experimenters have discovered that even rats who are stuffed will eat more if they're offered a new food.

Turn the lights down low

• *Snackers in* one experiment ate twice as many nuts when they were spotlighted as when they were dimly lit. (Besides, dim lights may lead to romance. And who thinks about food then?)

Depressing your appetite

• *Twenty minutes* before you eat, have an acidic food or drink, like grapefruit or tomato juice. Acids stimulate an intestinal hormone that tells the brain when you're full.

• *Or, start* the meal with a cup of soup (not the creamy kind, of course; broth is best). People who do tend to eat fewer calories at the meal.

• *And tighten* your belt. It's been established that feeling increased pressure will keep you from eating too much.

Low-calorie brown-bagging

• *Try whipping* large-curd cottage cheese in your food processor, mixing it with chopped onion or scallions, thin radishes, parsley, and/or sprouts, and eating with melba toast. The Germans call this treat *quark*. I call it good.

• *Borrow a* trick from the Chinese and wrap your meal in a leaf of iceberg lettuce. Spread the leaves with mustard or low-cal mayonnaise, top with thin-sliced chicken, turkey, ham, or beef, or with cheese or vegetables. Roll up and pin with toothpicks.

• *Before making* a sandwich with a roll, pull out the doughy center. You won't miss it, but you'll save a lot of calories.

• *You'll keep* your lunch crisper if you pack greens and dressings separately and toss just before eating.

• *If you're* tired of green salad, have pasta for a change. One-half cup of cooked macaroni has only seventy-eight calories. Toss it with a low-cal dressing and add chopped celery and peppers.

• *If you* eat your "sandwich" in two parts—a scoop of filling on lettuce, plus bread on the side—it will take you longer to eat, and you may find it more satisfying.

Tilt!
• *If you* can't read the numbers on your scale, just put a magnifying glass over the dial. Even if you don't believe the numbers, at least you'll be able to see them.

MAKING CALORIES COUNT

Trimming fat calories
• *Cut the* calories in meat loaf by placing it on a small cake rack. Then place the rack into a pan. The meat will brown on all sides and fat will drip off. (Draining one pound of cooked ground beef removes 290 calories).
• *Brown hamburger* meat in the microwave in a microwave safe colander and drain off fat. Use the less fat meat in spaghetti sauce, chili, etc.
• *Make soups* and stews a day ahead and refrigerate. Remove congealed fat before you serve them. Each tablespoon you remove means 117 calories less in the serving dish.
• *The longer* you cook fatty meats, the less fat is left. Dieters should order meat medium to well-done.

Skinning the bird
• *Discarding the* skin of cooked poultry will cut fat calories in half. Use a paper towel instead of a knife to remove it. The towel grabs much better.

Gravy with fewer calories.
• *Thicken with* cornstarch instead of flour. Cornstarch has the same calories as flour but twice the thickening power, so you'll use less.

Watching your spread
• *Try cutting* down the amount of butter the recipe calls for. You probably won't even notice the difference.
• *Don't kid* yourself into thinking that margarine has fewer calories than butter. Both have about 124 per tablespoon.
• *Butter toast* cold and you'll use less. Warm toast absorbs more.
• *Similarly, slice* English muffins, don't pull them apart. You can spread less butter on the flatter surface.

Water for dieters
• *Dieters who* drink lots of water lose weight better and more consistently than those who don't. It's nature's diuretic.
• *Try drinking* a glass of water when you feel hungry between meals. Doctors have found that very often people confuse hunger with thirst.

Alcoholic calories
• *It's the* proof that's important, not how sweet it is. One and a half ounces of seventy-nine proof whiskey is eighty-five calories. One-hundred-proof whiskey has 125.

COOKING WITH FEWER CALORIES

Eggs
• *Separate eggs,* beat the egg whites until stiff, and fold into batter to increase the volume of dessert.
• *Use no-cholesterol* egg substitute in place of eggs. You'll save about forty-five calories per egg.

Milk and cream
• *Blender-whip low-fat,* part-skim ricotta cheese with skim milk to make a cream substitute in sauces and batters.
• *Use evaporated* milk instead of cream and save 733 calories per cup.
• *You can* even whip evaporated skim milk in place of whipped cream if you chill milk, bowl, and beaters very well; beat in one tablespoon lemon juice for added firmness; sweeten to taste.

Sour cream
• *Use plain* low-fat yogurt instead of sour cream and save 350 calories per cup.
• *Or blend* one cup low-fat cottage cheese, two teaspoons skim milk, and two teaspoons lemon juice.
• *Or blender-whip* cottage cheese thinned with buttermilk.

For cream cheese
• *Blender-whip fresh* farmer cheese smooth as a substitute for cream cheese in cheesecakes. Omit lemon juice.
• *Or, use* cottage cheese, blender-whipped until all graininess disappears.
• *Or, replace* it with lower-calorie Neufchâtel cheese.

For nuts
- *Use nutty* or crunchy cereals instead.
- *Use walnut* flavoring in batters to increase nutty taste.
- *Use peanut* butter in place of part of the shortening and you'll need fewer additional nuts for taste.

SWEET SUGGESTIONS FOR THE DIETER

"Home-made" low-calorie gelatin
- *Substitute one* envelope of plain gelatin and two cups of fruit juice for low-calorie gelatin without extra chemicals. First soften the gelatin granules in a little cold fruit juice, then warm just enough to dissolve completely.

"Home-made" diet soda
- *Use a* tablespoon or two of defrosted juice concentrate in each glassful of club soda or seltzer with ice.

Reduced-calorie pie
- *Make pies* with only a single crust and save eight hundred calories. Put the crust on the bottom and cover the filling with foil during baking. Or put the crust on top and serve the "pie" cobbler style.
- *Roll pie* pastry very, very thin. For frozen, ready-to-bake pastry, defrost, cover with waxed paper, roll until fifty percent wider, trim, and discard extra pastry.
- *Or simply* transfer defrosted, unbaked pie shells to larger pans and stretch to fit with fingertips.

Cutting down on sugar
• *Use more* vanilla than called for. It increases the sensation of sweetness.
• *Defrosted juice* concentrate (fifteen calories per tablespoon) can be used as sugarless jam or sauce.
• *Add "sweet"* spices such as ginger, cardamom, cloves, cinnamon, nutmeg, and allspice, and you can cut down on sugar.
• *Overripe fruit* is naturally sweet and is usually bargain priced. Blender-whip it into a fruit puree that you can store in the freezer to use as a sauce.
• *If you* reduce the sour and bitter ingredients, you can cut the amount of sugar in a recipe; for example, use less lemon juice, or substitute milk chocolate for dark.
• *Broiling grapefruit,* banana, onions, or tomatoes, or letting the water cook out of carrots, will caramelize the natural sugars.

Using sugar substitutes
• *You can* make up for the lost volume from sugar that's left out by beating egg whites or yolks until stiff.
• *The more* baking powder or yeast a recipe calls for, the more it will compensate for the lack of volume from the omitted sugar.

 **GETTING A MOVE ON**

Shaping up means moving out

• *The fewer* meals a person eats, the greater his tendency to obesity. Obese teen girls in one study actually ate less in crash diet efforts than girls of normal weight. But, since they were poorly fueled, they were sluggish and spent nearly five hours more a day sleeping or sitting than their thin friends. That put the weight on.

How much to exercise

• *Aerobic activity* such as walking, running, skipping rope, riding an exercycle, dancing, lowers your risk of heart attack by strengthening your heart and lungs and building endurance.

• *To be* aerobic, an exercise should be done continuously for fifteen to twenty minutes without a break, after ten minutes of warm-up and followed by ten minutes of cool-down.

• *Exercising less* than three times a week is virtually useless. Exercising four times a week is three times as effective as exercising three times a week, according to one study.

Stretch it out

• *Don't start* your stretching until after you've warmed up your tissues with five to ten minutes of steadily increasing exercise such as walking, jogging, or bicycling. When you're warm, your body is more supple, less prone to injury.

• *Do your* stretches slowly and with slowly increasing intensity. Sudden and violent stretching can weaken muscles and possibly damage them.

Don't bounce
• *"Bouncing" stretch* exercises used to be a standard part of most warm-up routines. However sports doctors now think this may actually cause muscles to tense up. Slow stretching, using your body weight and gravity, is best.

Taking it to the limit
• *All older* folks who exercise are healthier than sedentary types, but competitive types have an extra edge. Elderly joggers who continue to train for competition age far more slowly than those who exercise casually. But of course check with your doctor before beginning any exercise program.
• *The exercising* repetitions that come after you are ready to give up are the ones that increase muscle size and strength. (That's what they mean by "No pain, no gain.") Knowing that may help you keep going.

How hard to exercise
• *Subtract your* age from 220 and you'll get your maximum heart rate. Try to get your pulse rate to seventy or seventy-five percent of that figure during exercise—but check with your doctor to make sure which resting and exercising rates are appropriate for you.

Checking your pulse
• *Press the* middle three fingers of one hand against the opposite wrist and feel for the pulse. Count the number of beats for six seconds, then multiply that number by ten.

In a walk
• *Nothing improves* overall health (including circulation) better than brisk walking.

• *Brisk walking* (three and a half to five mph) may burn as much as eighty-one percent of the calories burned in running, and fast walking (five mph or more) actually burns one hundred more calories than jogging at the same rate because you exert more energy taking strides than you do running.

• *Walking a* mile in eight minutes burns the same calories as jogging a mile in eight and a half minutes.

• *There is* only one-third of the pressure on the body when walking as compared to running, and less chance of back, joint, and muscle injury.

Walking the right way

• *You should* aim for a pace of at least three mph for forty minutes—plus ten minutes of warm-up and ten cooling down.

• *Don't bounce* up and down. Walk briskly, swing arms naturally, keep your body relaxed—but feel the push.

• *And keep* at it. The point is to make the exercise continuous, so window-shopping doesn't count (except in your pocketbook, if you're lured inside the store).

Jumping for joy

• *Jumping rope* is probably the most convenient exercise, since you can do it right at home. It's certainly the most efficient. Ten minutes of jumping equals thirty minutes of jogging.

• *If you're* older or out of shape, try jumping one foot at a time for an easier pace.

• *Trying to* increase the benefit of jumping rope? Don't do it by jumping faster. Just lift your feet higher.

Exercises for the desk set
• *If you've* been sitting too long, relax your body and stretch. Start by spreading knees slightly, dropping head and arms between them. Count five beats, then slowly pull yourself upright using the muscles in your lower back.
• *Rotate wrists* and ankles for a couple of minutes once or twice each hour.
• *Place palms* of your hands on the desktop and slowly lift one leg at a time while keeping your back pressed against the chair. You'll keep stomach muscles firm, reduce lower back pain.

Lose twelve pounds without dieting
• *If you* climb two more flights of stairs a day, you'll burn enough calories to lose twelve pounds a year.

Easing the pain
• *Rest, Ice,* Compression, Elevation—the "RICE" cure—is the remedy for a turned ankle or twisted knee.
• *Apply an* ice pack for twenty to thirty minutes, every couple of hours. In between, wrap the area snugly with an elastic bandage to help reduce swelling. (Be sure the wrap is tighter below the joint or bruise, and looser on top, so blood is forced to the heart and excess fluid is forced away from the injury.)
• *Keep the* injury elevated—above the level of your heart, if possible.

Cast aside
• *To help* casts slide into clothing more easily, use an old pair of panty hose. Snip off the panty and feet portions, and slip the remaining leg portion over the arm or leg cast.

STRESSFUL CONDITIONS

That lump in your throat
• *It could* be a response to stress. Try breathing slowly and deeply so the muscles that cause that sensation will unclench and relax.

Stomach "in knots"
• *Studies have* shown that stress slows down food digestion, so there's some truth to the saying about a stomach being "all tied up in knots." If that's how yours feels at the end of a hectic day, take ten to fifteen minutes just before a meal to sip a glass of water slowly . . . and *relax*.

What to eat in time of stress
• *Don't turn* to pacifiers like sweets. If you're having a rough time, your body loses its reserves of vitamins A and C faster than it normally would, so eat foods packed with these nutrients: dark green and yellow vegetables for A; citrus fruits, baked potato, strawberries, and green peppers for C.
• *Also take* in proteins, especially milk products, which contain riboflavin and calcium.

Coloring your behavior
• *Researchers think* that different colors can cause different behavior reactions in yourself and others. For example, certain shades of pink may act as a sedative and possibly even relax muscles. The brain reacts to pink by slowing the release of adrenaline into your system, which in turn slows the heart muscle and calms you down. So if you're planning to ask your boss for a raise, wear pink.

VISITING THE DOCTOR

Less waiting time
• *You're less* likely to be sitting around the waiting room with rising blood pressure if you choose appointments at these times:

> Lunch hours (all doctors)
> Tuesdays or Thursdays for general practitioners
> December for dentists
> Midwinter or early spring for eye doctors
> Evenings for pharmacists
> Midsummer and Friday afternoons for gynecologists

YOUR MEDICINE

Tough pill to swallow
• *The American* Medical Association says to swallow a tablet by placing it on the tongue, sipping water, and tilting your head back.
• *With a* capsule, tilt head forward while swallowing. The capsule weighs less than water, so the forward motion will flush it down your throat.

To get medicine down, stand up
• *If you* take medication while you're lying down, you may delay its entry into your bloodstream and cause yourself nausea and heartburn if it remains in your esophagus. Unless you're confined to bed, stand up to swallow and remain standing for ninety seconds.
• *And always* take tablets or capsules with at least

one full glass of fluid. This is especially important with aspirin, to minimize stomach irritation. (It also helps to take aspirin immediately after a meal.)

YOUR ACHING HEAD

Ten kinds of headaches you may never have known you had

- *Chinese restaurant* syndrome: Comes from too much monosodium glutamate in your food—Chinese or other kinds.
- *Hot dog* headache: From nitrates or nitrites added to hot dogs, ham, bacon. If you boil these meats, the additives dissolve.
- *Ice-cream headache:* From sudden cooling of the roof of the mouth, which affects the nerves. Eat cold foods slowly.
- *Caffeine withdrawal:* If you're used to caffeine, blood vessels are constricted. Take it away quickly, and they dilate. Withdraw slowly to avoid a headache.
- *Hunger headache:* From not eating enough, or from eating too much. Excess sweets may cause your pancreas to create a lot of insulin, and your blood sugar becomes too low. Snack on high-protein foods instead (nuts, fruits, vegetables).
- *Noxious fumes* headache: From crowded highways; also from formaldehyde, found in plywood and home insulating materials.
- *Bruxism headache:* From grinding your teeth at night, or from excessive gum chewing.
- *Turtle headache:* If you sleep with the covers over your head, you build up carbon dioxide (or you can get it from a crowded room). Tuck covers in so you

can't pull them up. Or if you're doing it to avoid light, try wearing a sleep mask.

- *Sunstroke headache:* The body is dehydrated from the sun, so drink small amounts of warm water over a two- or three-hour period.
- *Salt: Stay* away from highly salted snack foods.

Cure for a leaky ice bag

- *Fit a* plastic bag into the ice bag, fill, and tie the plastic bag closed before you cap the bag. You've got an ice bag within an ice bag and no leaks.

JUST THE (COLD) FACTS

Hot foods for cold

- *Mother was* right: take chicken soup—or any hot liquid—when you've got a cold. Hot liquids increase mucus flow, which helps end the infection more quickly.
- *Or, eat* something really hot, such as horseradish, chili, mustard, or pepper.
- *Or, gargle* with ten to twenty drops of Tabasco sauce in a glass of water. You'll clear out the respiratory tract.

Keeping colds away

- *Washing your* hands often may keep you free of sniffles, since colds may be contracted by touching the skin of an infected person. So keep your hands clean and avoid rubbing your eyes and nose.

Holidays and illness

- *Christmas and* New Year's are traditional peak times for catching cold, because you're in crowded rooms with poor circulation and because you're under stress, which helps increase your susceptibility. Try to get as much rest as possible.

- *If you* get an annual *cold* around the holidays (runny nose, itchy eyes, hoarseness) you may just be allergic to your Christmas tree (four million people are). To test, stow your tree outdoors for a couple of days. If the *cold* disappears, go for the fabulous fake next year.

An accurate temperature

- *Put the* thermometer way back under the tongue. That's where the heat pockets are that best reflect your temperature.

Let me feel your forehead

- *Don't just* touch hands to the forehead of someone who may have a temperature. Touch both your hands *and* your face, then touch a well person for comparison.
- *If the* patient is a child, touch your hands and your face to both his forehead and his stomach, then touch a well person.
- *But remember:* This is only a rough gauge of temperature.

Coughing is good for you

- *It may* make you uncomfortable, but it's nature's way of clearing the air passages. It's best not to suppress it. To simply soothe your throat: honey (lots of it) in tea is good.

Be a sourpuss when you have a cough

- *Feed your* face a pickle, some lemon—anything acidic. Acids help promote the flow of saliva that helps the cough.

• *And drink* lots of water. It helps liquefy phlegm, making it easier to cough up.

Sweet advice for sore throats

• *Try a* tablespoon of honey and vinegar mixed into your tea. The honey will help soothe the sore throat and relieve coughing, and the vinegar helps break up mucus.

Drag yourself around

• *Even a* short period of bed rest can cause dramatic deconditioning. Muscles start to atrophy, bones lose calcium, your blood pressure goes down, and dehydration occurs. So stay as active as you can: don't take to your bed unless you're really ill. You'll be back to your old self faster if you get up as soon as possible.

UNDER THE SUN

Bad skin needs sunscreen

• *Sun doesn't* help acne. It actually causes skin to thicken, which could cause more blackheads.

Think ahead

• *Sunscreen gives* you maximum protection if you apply it at least thirty minutes before going out.

Even out the tan

• *Changing swimsuit* styles in midsummer can leave your back looking like a patchwork quilt. Don't despair: Use sunscreen on the tanned areas and quick-tanning lotion on pale ones. They should balance out in a few days.

Sunburn without sun
• *Since ultraviolet* light penetrates clouds, bounces off sand and pavement, you should be cautious about exposure. So don't forget to use sunscreen on cloudy days, too.
• *Even being indoors* in a car leaves you vulnerable. Men most often get skin cancer on the left, women on the right, presumably because that's where they sit in the car. So use sunscreen on all exposed skin.

Sunburn relievers
• *To cool* down affected areas, rub with apple cider vinegar.
• *Pat with* a wet tea bag.
• *Or,* apply a paste of baking soda and water.

Water near the brain?
• *Here's a* great way to get rid of plugged ears from swimming. Tilt the ear with the water in it toward the floor, then jump up on the corresponding foot—right ear, right foot; left ear, left foot. The ear will immediately unplug. Don't laugh. It works!

STOMACH PROBLEMS

Diet for an upset stomach
• *Drink lots* of water and flat, non-cola, non-diet soft drinks. Sugar in them stimulates stomach activity.

• *Or, eat* dry foods like unbuttered toast and plain popcorn. They stimulate stomach activity, too.
• *It's better* to eat small, frequent meals until you feel right again.
• *If you're* nauseated, try sucking on ice cubes or chips.

Tips for heartburn sufferers
• *Lying down* makes the condition worse.
• *Drinking milk* offers temporary relief, but within an hour the calcium causes the stomach to produce more acid. Avoid it.
• *Eating smaller*, more frequent meals (five rather than three) may reduce pressure in the stomach.
• *Avoid regular* and even decaffeinated coffee. The caffeine alone increases acid production, and an ingredient in the coffee itself stimulates even more.

WITHSTANDING WINTER

Dressing for the cold
• *If the* temperature is thirty-six degrees, with a windchill factor of minus fifteen degrees, dress for fifteen-degree weather.
• *Wear three* layers: The innermost should be absorbent, with a sweatshirt of natural material on top, followed by a windbreaker of cotton (allows sweat to evaporate). Below twenty degrees, add an insulating layer like a turtleneck under the sweatshirt.
• *A hat's* a must. Most blood vessels contract to save heat in cold weather, but the blood vessels in the head

The Well Worker

211

stay open to keep blood going to the brain. That's why you lose fifty percent of body heat through your head.

- *For coldest* weather, wear long underwear under your pants.
- *Mittens are* warmer than gloves, since they have less surface area to lose heat. In a pinch, ball up your hands within the mittens.
- *Two pairs* of thin socks insulate better than one pair of thick ones.
- *Wear shoes* loose enough so they don't cut off the flow of blood. The blood helps keep feet warm.

To keep your mood light
- *Winter depression* may be associated with increased production of a hormone called melatonin, which your body produces when light is restricted. Remedy: More exposure to ultraviolet rays.
- *Try opening* windows (glass filters out most ultraviolet rays).
- *Go without* sunglasses at least part of the time.
- *Go on* a brief walk at noon when the sun is brightest.

THE WELL WORKER

For more comfort at your desk
- *Put a* phone book underneath and prop your feet on it. This will help relieve pressure on your lower back.
- *Distribute your* weight evenly by sitting on both hips at the same time.

• *Put a* pillow on the back of your chair, right below your shoulder blades.

• *If you* must lean over your work, don't hunch your back and shoulders. Instead, bend from your hip sockets.

• *Don't twist* your torso toward your work; face it head-on.

• *Empty your* back pockets. Sitting on bulky objects can put pressure on the sciatic nerves in your legs.

• *Always keep* your feet on the floor or on a book for support.

• *Always sit* with your knees slightly higher than your hips. Otherwise, your lower back will be stressed.

• *Stand up* from your desk, stretch, and walk around as often as you can.

If the chair fits

• *You'll work* better. People in ill-fitting chairs lose an average of forty minutes of work time daily.

• *The test* of a good chair: Can you sit with calves and thighs at right angles? Is your torso tilted back slightly, with support in the small of the back? If not, ask for a new chair.

Quick stress relievers on the job

• *Find an* empty office and lie down on the carpeted floor. Bend your knees, bring them to your chest, and clasp your hands around them. Gently rock back and forth. Breathe deeply. This will make you feel much better. (Unless you haven't locked the door and your boss stumbles over you!)

• *Or, stand* in a doorway, pressing one palm against each door frame. Hold your breath and increase pressure until you feel warmth coming to your neck, face, and head. Hold for as long as you can, then release and inhale deeply. Repeat this three times.

Start fidgeting
• *Sitting too* long causes swelling in ankles and feet. Do what kids do naturally: squirm, kick your legs, roll your ankles, roll your head around, wring your arms, wrap your arms around your chest.

Pull up a piece of the floor
• *Try sitting* on the floor for a while each day. It exercises your ball-and-socket hip joint, which never gets worked out if you always sit in a chair.

An out-of-sight exercise
• *If you're* desk-bound, try slipping off your shoes and rubbing your feet on a rolling pin under the desk. It improves circulation.

A GOOD NIGHT'S REST

Beddy buys
• *Test a* mattress by sitting on the edge, then getting up. A good one resumes its shape immediately.
• *And lie* on the bed, roll to the edge. It should support you, shouldn't tip or sag.
• *And check* that the mattress supports your shoulders and hips without sagging.

Windows—open or closed?
• *Couples who* constantly battle over this issue may reach a truce if they know that you sleep more soundly in a cool room with plenty of ventilation.
• *But in* coldest weather, keep windows closed.

Freezing air has too little moisture and brings the humidity (and therefore the comfort level) too far down.

Caffeine keeping you awake?

• *Peak stimulation* may occur two to four hours after you've drunk coffee, causing you to awaken at night or too early in the morning. If you can't nod off, break the late-night coffee habit.

• *Cut down* on caffeine in tea by shortening brewing time. Brewing one minute can result in as little as nine mg. caffeine, but steep the tea five minutes and your cup will have thirty mg. of caffeine or more.

• *Reduce the* effect of tannic acid by adding milk to the tea.

Insomnia beater

• *It really* is true: Milk works. That's because it contains a substance that is converted into a brain chemical that works like a sedative. So try a glass of warm milk, or yogurt, or a couple of calcium tablets if you're having trouble dropping off.

Zzzz!

• *People snore* only when they're lying on their backs—so keep your snorer on his side or stomach this way: put a marble in a piece of cheesecloth and sew it to the back of his pajamas between the shoulder blades. When he rolls on his back, he'll feel uncomfortable and he'll change position.

WHATEVER AILS YOU

Hiccups
• *Swallow a* teaspoonful of dry granulated sugar and they'll go away. This is great to know when kids are hiccuping (use a smaller amount with an infant).
• *Or, try* saturating a lemon wedge in Angostura bitters and eating the entire wedge (but not the rind).

Poison ivy
• *Pour two* cups of milk into a quart container, then fill it up by adding ice cubes plus two tablespoons of salt. Apply to infected area with a cloth for twenty minutes, three or four times daily. This works for bug bites and sunburn, too.

DID YOU KNOW...

How to tell if you're well balanced
• *To pass* the civilian pilot medical exam, you must be able to stand with feet together without swaying for ten seconds with your eyes closed.
• *And (also* with eyes closed) hold your arms straight out at shoulder height and touch your toes with alternating hands.
• *Military pilots* must be able to do all of the above, plus walk a perfectly straight line with eyes closed, and do ten or twelve knee bends.

15

Best of Helpful Hints for Kids

BABY TALK

Special introduction

• *Before going* to the hospital to have another baby, wrap a gift for your older child. Take it to the hospital and send it home with a snapshot and a greeting from the new baby. No one likes to feel left out.

Bedtime

• *A standard-sized* pillowcase will cover the pad in a bassinet. In case of late-night accidents, turn the pad over to the fresh, clean side.

• *Use two* or more crib sheets with rubberized flannel pads in between when making up the crib. When baby's bed needs changing, remove the top sheet and pad.

• *Pet-proof the* nursery by installing a screen door and you'll still be able to hear what's going on.

Bottles

• *Speed up* heating water for baby's late-night bottle

by filling an airpot or Thermos with boiling water before going to bed.

• *Rid sour* milk smells from plastic bottles by filling the bottle with warm water and adding one teaspoon of baking soda. Shake well and let set overnight.

• *Save a* couple of empty soft drink cartons and use them to hold baby bottles in the refrigerator. The bottles can easily be removed for access to anything stored behind.

Making a traveling bed for baby

• *If you* are traveling with a small baby and do not want to haul a crib, simply use a small, inflatable plastic pool and blow up. Cover with a sheet and secure the ends underneath.

• *Or take* along a heavy-duty, flat cardboard box. Set up the box on the floor and line the bottom with a heavy, quilted blanket. The high sides will keep drafts off baby.

The baby and the bathwater

• *Use baby's* infant seat for bathing in the bathtub. Remove the pad and buckle strap and place a large folded bath towel on the seat and on the bathtub floor (to prevent slipping). Place baby in seat, and run water into tub. Now you can use both hands.

• *When a* child is past the baby stage, but is too small for the tub, get a plastic clothes basket with holes in it. Place the basket in several inches of tub water and set your child inside. Never leave child unattended.

• *Put small* pieces of soap into a white sock and tie up the open end. Children prefer it to a bar of soap and it will not slip from their hands.

• *With a* bath towel wrapped around your neck and pinned on like a bib, you'll keep dry during the bath.

It also makes an instant wrap-up for baby.

• *Don't startle* an infant with cold baby lotion. Warm it first by setting the lotion bottle in a pan of hot water.

Helping the medicine go down

• *Even the* worst-tasting medicines go down without fuss when you put the prescribed amount in a nipple, then give it to baby just before feeding time. He'll be so hungry he'll scarcely realize he has swallowed it.

• *Give liquid* vitamins at bath time. No more stained clothing to launder.

Safe and sound

• *When your* child reaches the creeping stage, tape light cords tightly around a table leg. This will prevent him from pulling lamps onto the floor. If you use transparent tape, it will not mar the furniture.

• *Keep a* tray of juice-flavored ice cubes on hand when baby is learning to walk. If she falls and bumps her lip, let her suck on the flavored cube to reduce the swelling. It tastes so good she might forget about the fall.

Read all about it

• *Haven't had* the time to read the newspaper because baby is fussy? Read it aloud while rocking her. She'll think you are talking to her and enjoy it as much as a lullaby.

Weighing in with baby

• *Here's how* to watch your own weight while keeping track of baby's. Get on the bathroom scale alone, then weigh yourself while holding baby in your arms. Baby's weight is the difference between the two.

OPEN UP WIDE

Introducing solid food
• *The baby* will be more likely to eat a new food when he's the hungriest, so feed it to him at the start of a meal.

"Bib-bits"
• *If you* tuck a sponge in the pocket of a plastic bib, it'll stay open wide enough to catch any spilled liquids.
• *Safety-pin the* bottom of the bib to baby's clothes for lots better coverage.

Sitting pretty in the high chair
• *Use bath* towels to pad the back of the high chair. The towels will also add back support while she sits.
• *Or put* a thick foam rubber cushion on the high chair seat. The cushion also helps keep spilled liquids from dripping onto the floor.
• *Put newspaper* down underneath, instead of plastic. You'll save time by throwing away the mess instead of scrubbing it up.

Avoiding falls
• *Prevent baby's* high chair from tipping over by screwing a screen-door fastener to the wall. Attach the hook to the back of the high chair and latch the chair to the wall.
• *Put a* small rubber mat—the type you would use in the sink—on the seat of the high chair to keep baby from sliding out.

High chair cleanup
• *The best* place to clean a high chair is outdoors—
with a garden hose.
• *In winter*, place it under the shower and let hot
water spray over it for several minutes.

Eliminating milk spills
• *Your child* will be able to hold onto a glass of milk
better if you place two tight rubber bands around the
glass an inch or so apart. This makes it easier for little
hands to hold.

    TODDLING ALONG

Fast foods
• *An egg* poacher is ideal for warming several foods
at once.

Cutting down on sugar
• *Prevent the* kids from sprinkling too much sugar on
cereal by keeping the sugar in a salt shaker.

Be a good example
• *A simple* rule that will save a lot of discipline in the
future is: Never do anything with a child that must be
corrected later. For example, don't stand a child on a
chair or bed while dressing her. Later she must learn
not to stand on the furniture.

Baby's first pair of shoes
• *For baby's* first pair of hard-soled shoes, walking on
a hard surface is like walking on ice for an adult. If

you glue a very thin strip of foam rubber to the soles of the shoes, the baby will gain confidence when he is walking. When foam rubber is worn, scrape off the remains with a razor blade and apply a new piece.

Put the squeeze on it
• *Little children* love to watch a new roll of toilet tissue spin off the roll. To prevent roll-offs, before inserting it on the holder, squeeze the roll together so it's no longer round.

Safety measures
• *Perhaps your* child, when riding her tricycle on your driveway, rides too close to the street for safety. A white line painted across the driveway at a safe distance from the street might help. Tell her it's the finish line and she's not to go any farther.
• *Hang a* towel over the top of the bathroom door to prevent lock-ins.
• *Even adults* sometimes walk into sliding glass doors. To help the youngsters avoid this hazard, place a piece of colored tape on the glass at eye level to alert the child when the door is closed.
• *To protect* your child from mashed fingers, place a cork at each end of the keyboard on the piano. Now, if the lid drops, his fingers are saved.

Making a door for baby
• *Attach an* extra handle near the bottom of the screen door. Your child will then be able to pull the door open himself without calling for help.

Comforting suggestions
• *Clean a* cut or scrape with a red washcloth. The blood won't show and the child won't be frightened.
• *Don't apply* salve or liquid antiseptic directly to a

cut. It's less traumatic if it's put on the bandage before applying it to the skin.

• *If you* can't see the splinter in a finger, touch the
spot with iodine. The splinter will darken and be easier to locate.

• *When bathing* a child, keep a plaster cast dry by
covering it with a plastic bag secured with waterproof
electrical tape.

• *Give your* child an ice cube to suck on before giving
her bitter-tasting medicine. Her taste buds will be de-
sensitized and medicine will go down a bit easier.

Easy eyedrop application

• *Have the* child lie down and close his eyes, then
place the eyedrops in the corner of each eye. As he
opens them, the drops spread gently throughout.

In the sickbed

• *Make a* table for a child who's spending the day in
bed: use an adjustable ironing board.

• *To help* eliminate spills, place a damp washcloth
under the plate on a tray for serving children in bed.

• *When using* a cool-mist vaporizer, the stream of
cool mist can be directed where you want it if you
tape a three-foot (or more) piece of vent pipe to the
vaporizer opening.

Removing gum from hair

• *Rub ordinary* cold cream into the hair. Pull down on
the strands of hair several times with a dry towel.

• *Or, rub* in a dab of peanut butter. Massage the gum
and peanut butter between your fingers until the gum
is loosened. Remove with facial tissue.

• *Or apply* Spray 'n' Wash generously to the gum,

then rub hair between fingers. Comb the gum out, then wash the child's hair.
• *"Freeze"* the hair with ice cubes and peel gum off.

TEACHING WITHOUT PREACHING

Disciplinary actions
• *You have* trouble getting your children into the tub? Tell them that the last one to take a bath must clean it.
• *If you* have trouble getting them out, pull the plug.
• *If you* can't seem to get your kids to clean up after themselves, hide everything you pick up in a secret place and charge a dime an item as ransom.
• *To train* children not to complain or tattle, give them a limited supply of "complaint tickets." Each time they have a complaint, they must give you a ticket before you will listen. The child will have to think twice before using up one of his complaints.
• *If children* argue over who gets the largest portion when sharing a treat, let one child divide the treat while the other selects his/her portion first.

Be prepared!
• *Play the* "what if" game with kids. Give them situations to solve, like getting separated from you at the department store, and ask them what they would do. If they answer correctly, praise them. If they don't know what to do, here's the perfect chance to talk things out with them—for their safety and your peace of mind.

Telling right from left
• *Do your* children have a hard time remembering right from left? Just have them extend the thumb and forefinger of both hands. The hand that makes an *L* is the left one.

Remembering address and phone number
• *Try setting* both to music. Kids will find important information easier to remember if it is set to a tune they can sing.

Practicing writing names
• *A preschooler* can learn to write his name correctly this way: write each letter of the name in dot-to-dot fashion on a small piece of cardboard. Cover with clear contact paper so your child has a washable surface to practice on.

Quick learners
• *Here's a* great way to teach a child the concept of time. If you plan a trip to the zoo in five days, for example, make a chain of five paper links and have him take one off every day.

Brushing teeth
• *If you* don't have time to watch the kids brushing, invest in a three-minute egg timer and tell them they have to keep brushing until the sands run out. Children think the timing's fun, and you'll know they're not rushing the job.

Filling the tub
• *If big* kids want to fill the tub to the top, prevent quarrels by sticking a decal on the side of the tub.

When water reaches the decal, they'll know it's time to turn the water off.

GETTING ORGANIZED

Where's the rubber ducky?
• *Purchase a* plastic bicycle basket. The handles fit perfectly over the bathtub soap dish. Toys can drain overnight, since the basket has an open weave.

Finding clothes faster
• *If two* kids of the same sex share the same closet, mark hanger tops with strips of tape in different colors.
• *Or buy* each child hangers in different colors.

Clock watchers
• *Kids won't* keep popping in and out of the house to find out the time if you put a clock in the window.

Look what's under the bed
• *An old* twin bed mattress makes an extra bed for sleep-over friends. Slide it under a bed for easy storage.

PLAYTIME

Recipes for play
• *Make fingerpaints* in your kitchen by mixing two

cups of cold water and one-quarter cup of cornstarch, then boil liquid until thick. Pour into smaller containers and color with various food colorings.

• *For a* great play dough for your children, mix one cup of salt and two cups of flour and add enough water to make a soft dough. Add any food coloring desired. Keep tightly sealed.

• *Make colorful* beads from cut macaroni by dunking them into assorted food colors. Drain and dry completely. Pour the beads into individual paper cups and let older children make their own necklaces.

Painting the town

• *Put a* teaspoon of food coloring in a bottle of water and let your kids spray designs on snow and snow-covered shrubbery.

• *Add a* few drops of food coloring to your child's bubble bath for a nice surprise.

Finger-paint protection

• *Always add* about one-quarter teaspoon of liquid dishwashing detergent to finger paints. It won't stop spills, but they'll be easier to clean.

• *The key* to cleaning these paints off washable fabric is to let them dry. Once dry, most of the paint can be brushed off and the material washed as usual. But remember not to machine-dry, because this will set any remaining stain.

• *For paint* on walls and woodwork, blot up as much as possible with a damp rag. Then gently rub the area with baking soda on a damp cloth.

Roll-on "paintbrush"

• *Pry the* top off a roll-on deodorant bottle and rinse

both parts. Fill the jar with thinned finger paint or poster paint and replace the top. (To remove the roll-on ball from the bottle, gently pry off the top with a nail file.)

Cleaning stuffed toys
• *Clean with* dry cornstarch. Rub in, let stand briefly and brush off.

Picture this
• *As the* children bring their school pictures home each year, put each one in a frame right in front of last year's picture. It's a safe place to store them, and you'll have fun looking at the whole series every year.

The guest of honor
• *The reward* for a good report card doesn't always have to be money. Bring out the good china and silverware, set the child's place at the head of the table, make a cake decorated with a candle for each *A* or *B*. He'll feel like a king.

Fun in the sun
• *If your* child's slide has lost its "slide," rub a sheet of waxed paper on it and watch him scoot.

Birthday place cards
• *Make your* own. Write each guest's name in chocolate on a cookie iced in white.
• *Or print* the name of each child on a paper cup to eliminate mix-ups.
• *Or stick* a balloon with a child's name on it to the back of each chair.

For the cake

• *Use small* marshmallows as candle holders for a birthday cake. They prevent the wax drippings from running into the frosting.

• *Or use* Life Savers.

Cone sealers

• *To prevent* ice cream from leaking through the bottom of a cone, put a marshmallow on the bottom.

• *Or use* a dab of peanut butter.

Cake in a cone

• *Prepare your* favorite cake mix according to directions. Fill flat-bottomed ice-cream cones half full with batter and arrange on a cookie sheet. Bake at 350° for twenty minutes, cool, and add a scoop of ice cream.

CLOTHES ENCOUNTERS

Tongue-tied

• *To prevent* the tongues of your child's shoes from sliding out of place, cut two small, parallel slits in each tongue one-half inch from the outside tip. After lacing, pull through the new slots and tie as usual.

Winter wear

• *To store* mittens and stocking hats in one place, hang a shoe bag on the inside of the closet door nearest the entrance.

• *Sew a* loop of elastic into the cuffs of sweaters to keep the sleeves from pushing up when kids put on their coats. Be sure it isn't too tight.

• *Attach some* sort of trinket to a snowsuit zipper. It will be easier to identify and the snowsuit will zip up without a struggle.

• *Recycle an* old heavy sweater by turning it into mittens. Place your child's wrist on the waist ribbing and trace his hand. Cut around the thumb and hand outline, using double thickness. Stitch together, press, and you've got new mittens for nothing.

Grow-along clothes

• *Cut off* worn or too short sleeves from padded jackets to make a vest.

• *Buttoning clothes* will be easier if all the buttons are sewn on with elastic thread.

Ideas "to boot"

• *To avoid* lost boots, cut two matching shapes of colored tape and stick on the backs of each boot heel. Your child can easily spot them, even in a jumble of thirty pairs at school.

• *Putting snow* boots on over tennis shoes can be a real struggle. It's simple if you slip plastic bags over the tennis shoes before sliding the boots on.

AND AWAY WE GO

At the restaurant

• *Don't get* caught without a bib for very young children. Just carry a sweater chain in your purse and use it to clip a napkin around your child's neck.

At a friend's house

• *If you're* visiting with a very young child, protect

your friend's bedding when putting him down to nap. Double a sheet of aluminum foil and put it under the sheet or towel where baby will be napping. The foil keeps bed dry and also warms it to body temperatures.

At the beach

• *Bring along* a playpen without the floor. Set it on the sand so young ones can play safely without wandering off. (Works at picnic sites, too.)

• *Carry beach* toys in a plastic laundry basket so you can easily rinse off all the sand from them when it's time to leave the beach. Just dunk the filled basket in the water.

Red Alert

• *For a* day at the fair or zoo, dress each child in brightly colored clothing (red is great) to help keep track of them.

Settling the seating dispute

• *When kids* fight about where to sit, have them draw straws to see who gets which seat.

Portable art cases

• *A covered* 9 X 13 inch cake pan is great for holding crayons, pencils, paper, and small toys for small children. Closed, the pan makes a good drawing board.

• *Or, hang* a shoe pouch on the coat hook in the car and fill the pouches with small toys, crayons, drawing pads, etc.

Taking your child's friend along

• *Have the* parents give you a certified letter (with signatures witnessed by a notary public) agreeing that you can authorize emergency medical treatment for the child in case of accident or illness.

When you fly with kids
• *Don't shush* the child if he's crying during takeoff or descent. His ears may be bothering him. Crying's the best thing, in fact, since it keeps his ears open.
• *To reduce* pressure on ears, wake baby to give him a bottle or pacifier at takeoff and landing.
• *Have hard* candy or gum ready for the older kids.
• *No child* with a cold or middle-ear infection should fly.

16

Best of
Helpful Hints
for the Kitchen

SHOPPING STRATEGIES

Clip Service
• *Here's how* to clip coupons without destroying the paper before everyone's read it. Clip only around three sides of the coupon. The last person to read the paper can pull the coupons out for you.

Follow the directions
• *Arrange coupons* by aisles in the supermarket and save time.

Pin up
• *Clip marketing* list to the supermarket cart with a clothespin.

Out of the bag
• *Instead of* carrying a calculator, just round off each item purchased to the nearest dollar and put a mark on your grocery list for each dollar. You'll tally up to within a dollar or two of your total bill. Sad, but true!

RECIPE KEEPING

File it away
• *When you* find a better recipe than the one in your cookbook, copy it onto a file card and tape it over the recipe in your book. This way, you can use the book's index to find your new, improved recipe.
• *Another trick* is to glue an envelope to the inside of the front cover to hold new recipe cards and newspaper clippings.

At a glance
• *Keep recipe* card upright by placing it in the tines of a fork and putting the fork handle in a glass. Carry the glass with you from counter to range as you cook.
• *Or hang* a permanent clamp inside—or even outside—a cupboard door, just for this purpose.
• *Or, if* you use a card-file box for recipes, glue a cork to the top of the box. Cut a slot across the top of the cork and simply insert the card you need to use in an upright position.

TOOLS OF THE TRADE

Beer can openers
• *The pointed* end is an excellent tool for deveining shrimp.
• *Or, use* on those hard-to-open paper boxes that don't "press" open as easily as they're supposed to.

Melon ballers

• *Form appetizer-sized* meatballs for parties. Dip the baller in cold water occasionally to keep meat from sticking.

• *Or, scoop* olives out of the jar without piercing them. Juices will be drained, too, as you lift the olives out.

• *Or, core* pear or apple halves.

Pizza cutter

• *Cut homemade* bar cookies to make nice, smooth squares in half the time.

• *Or, score* fudge.

Potato peelers

• *Use the* tip to pit cherries.

• *Or, cut* orange or lemon rind peels. They'll come off without the white membrane.

 AT YOUR SERVICE

For fine china

• *Before washing* fine china and crystal, place a towel on the bottom of the sink to act as a cushion.

• *To remove* coffee or tea stains and cigarette burns, rub the spot with a damp cloth dipped in baking soda.

• *Wash plates* in warm water, a mild detergent, and one-quarter cup of ammonia. Rinse very thoroughly.

Washup substitute
• *When out* of liquid dishwashing detergent, use a mild shampoo.
• *And save* time and money by using the cheapest brand of dishwashing detergent plus a few tablespoons of vinegar to wash dishes in your sink—it cuts the grease and lets dishes sparkle.

Silver
• *Here's an* amazing time-saver for polishing tarnished silver: line the bottom of a pan with a sheet of aluminum foil or use an aluminum pan. Add three tablespoons of baking soda or Spic 'n Span or Soilax to each quart of water used. Heat the water to almost boiling. Dip the silver into the water and let it remain until the tarnish disappears. The silver must touch the aluminum.
• *When using* silver polish, add a few drops of ammonia and watch the results.
• *If polishing* only a few pieces, try toothpaste.
• *Make sure* silver is dry before putting it away. It's best to leave it out for several hours after polishing or washing. Dampness can cause silver to rust, which appears as black spots.
• *Old powder* puffs that have been washed and fluffed in the dryer are great for cleaning silver.

Silver Do's
• *Do wash* silver as soon as possible after it's had contact with eggs, olives, salad dressings, vinegar, and foods heavily seasoned with salt. These foods, especially eggs and salt, cause silver to tarnish rapidly.
• *Do place* a piece of chalk in silver chest to absorb moisture and prevent tarnishing.

• *Do buy* silver cloth, the tarnish-retardant flannel, available at better fabric stores, and make your own bags for storing silver. You'll save those extra dollars.

Silver don'ts

• *Don't store* plated silver in newspaper. Printer's ink can remove the plating.
• *Don't use* rubber gloves when polishing silver, or fasten silver with rubber bands, or place near rubber —rubber darkens silver.

Make glasses perfectly clear

• *When fine* crystal stains or discolors, fill glasses with water and drop in a denture tablet. Let stand until discoloration disappears.
• *Or, mix* sand with denatured alcohol and swish it around the glass until the cloudiness is gone.

Glass actions

• *Never use* your dishwasher or hot water for washing fine glass, especially when it is gold-rimmed.
• *Never put* a delicate glass in water bottom side first. It can crack from sudden expansion. The most delicate glassware is safe if slipped in edgewise.
• *Keep crystal* shining by washing it in a sinkful of warm water and one-quarter cup of ammonia.
• *White distilled* vinegar is a must for rinsing crystal. Add one cup of vinegar to a sinkful of warm water.
• *Dry with* completely dry towels.
• *Or use* a chamois cloth. It eliminates all lime and water spots and polishes windows and mirrors, too.

Crack-proofing glass

• *To prevent* drinking glasses from cracking when filled with hot liquids, place new glasses in a large pot. Fill the pot with cold water so the water covers the glasses entirely. *Slowly* bring the water to a boil. Turn the heat off and let the water cool. The glasses will never crack from hot beverages.

These are sharp ideas

• *Got a* trusty but rusty old knife that won't come clean? Sprinkle an abrasive cleanser on a cork, then dampen lightly, and rub the cork against the knife. The cork's smooth surface makes for complete abrasion and the knife will look terrific.

• *To keep* stainless steel knives shiny and bright, rub them with a piece of lemon peel, then wash in sudsy water.

• *Or use* rubbing alcohol.

When "stainless" stains

• *You can* get rid of brownish stains on stainless steel by rubbing it with a dishcloth dipped in household ammonia.

• *Or try* oven cleaner. Be sure to rinse well.

Tine-y spots

• *Use a* pipe cleaner dipped in silver polish to remove tarnish from between the tines of silver forks.

Finishing up

• *Remove stains* from a non-stick finish utensil by boiling it in two tablespoons of baking soda and one cup of water for fifteen minutes. After the pan has been rinsed and dried, coat it with vegetable oil.

THE BIG PICTURE

Cupboards

• *Cold tea* is a good cleaning agent for woodwork of any kind.

• *Renovate cupboards* that have become faded in spots by rubbing and buffing shoe polish of the same color into the stained areas. Two or three different colors may be needed to accomplish the job.

Counters

• *To remove* juice, coffee, or tea stains, scrub them vigorously with a paste of baking soda and water. Let set for half an hour, then wipe paste up with a wet sponge.

• *Nicked Formica* counter tops can be touched up with matching crayon or paint.

• *Formica that's* become dull can be shined up with floor wax.

Oven

• *An inexpensive* oven cleaner: Set oven on "warm" for about twenty minutes, then turn it off. Place a small dish of full-strength ammonia on the top shelf. Put a large pan of boiling water on the bottom shelf and let it sit overnight. In the morning, stand back and open the oven. Let it air awhile before you wash it with soap and water. Even the hard, baked-on grease will wash off easily. For a badly stained oven, repeat the operation the next night. (Ammonia fumes are dangerous, so open the outside kitchen door before opening oven door. Do not use this hint in kitchens with inadequate ventilation.)

• *Put all* the removable parts of your stove into a

plastic garbage bag and pour in a couple of cups of ammonia. Seal the bag with a tie and leave outdoors for several hours. Rinse clean with the garden hose. No mess and no scrubbing. Try this trick to keep the chrome rings on electric ranges clean.

• *Before cleaning* the bottom of the oven on an electric stove, prop up the heating element with a few clip clothespins. It will be held high enough so you can get underneath to clean.

• *For lighter* cleaning, keep a spray bottle filled with one-half ammonia and one-half water. Spray the oven walls, close the door, wait until the dirt softens, then wipe clean.

• *After cleaning* with a commercial cleaner, dissolve all traces of grease with a paste of baking soda and water. Spread on the oven floor and walls. Wait a second, then wipe clean.

• *Following an* oven spill, sprinkle the area with salt immediately. When the oven is cool, brush off burned food and wipe with a damp sponge.

• *Or sprinkle* the oven bottom with automatic-dishwasher soap and cover with wet paper towels. Let this stand for a few hours.

Refrigerator

• *Add a* little baking soda to the soapy wash water to deodorize the inside of the refrigerator.

• *To prevent* mildew from forming, wipe refrigerator with vinegar. The acid effectively kills mildew fungi.

• *Test the* gasket of your fridge by closing a dollar bill in the door. If it slips out easily, you need a new one.

Freezer

• *After the* freezer has been defrosted, spray it with alcohol or vegetable-oil spray. The next time you defrost it, it will take less work.

Sink
• *When water* corrosion or mineral-deposit buildup is a problem, lay strips of paper toweling around faucets where lime has accumulated. Pour vinegar on the toweling, and leave it alone for one hour. Lime deposits will soften and be easy to remove.
• *For a* sparkling-white porcelain sink, place paper towels across the bottom of sink and saturate with household bleach. Let sit for half an hour or so.
• *Sprinkle automatic-dishwasher* crystals on a wet sponge and scrub. This also works well on bathtub rings.
• *To clean* porcelain surfaces, sprinkle cream of tartar on a damp cloth. This removes rust, too.
• *Or*, *to remove rust,* use a cloth dampened with lighter fluid. Wash sink and hands thoroughly afterward.
• *Cut off* the foot of a clean old nylon stocking, roll it up, and use it with cleansers for cleaning sinks without scratching.

Wall
• *After you* clean the painted wall behind your stove, apply a generous coating of furniture polish, then buff well. The next time you clean, grease spatters can be wiped away with a dry paper towel.

HERE AND THERE

Butcher blocks
• *To clean* butcher blocks, cutting boards and wooden rolling pins, wash, then dry with a cloth, then cover

with salt to draw moisture out of the wood. Treat with mineral oil to maintain surface.

• *But if* you want a cleaning that will prevent potentially dangerous bacteria from breeding, you have to cover it with bleach and salt, scrub it with a stiff brush, then rinse with very hot water, and wipe with a clean cloth. Repeat with each use.

• *Never use* lard, oil, or soap (which will be absorbed) or steel wool (which may splinter).

• *To remove* gummy dough, sprinkle salt on a wet sponge and start rubbing.

• *Scrape butcher* blocks and pastry boards with a plastic windshield scraper. It's easier to use than a knife and it won't mark the wood.

Chrome polish

• *To keep* chrome gleaming, polish with a soft cloth saturated with rubbing alcohol.

• *Or use* ammonia and hot water.

• *Or rub* with dry baking soda and a dry cloth.

• *Nail polish* remover is also excellent for cleaning chrome decorations and knobs, especially on stoves. Be sure that all units are off, and rinse all items well with water.

Across the (drain)board

• *Clean by* soaking in bleach and water.

• *Coat rubber* drainboard trays with a light film of furniture polish to prevent staining. It makes the tray easier to clean, too.

• *Remove hard* water stains by tilting up the low end of the board slightly and pouring one cup of white vinegar over the board. Let it set overnight and rub off with a sponge in the morning.

Some "tips" for rubber gloves
• *Before using* new gloves, turn them inside out and paint the fingertips with a few coats of nail polish. Your nails are less likely to poke holes.
• *If they* do, patch small holes and tears with waterproof tape. It works fine and cuts down on replacing gloves because of leaks due to holes.

Pot holders
• *If sprayed* heavily with spray starch, pot holders will stay clean longer.

Shelf covering
• *To remove* old Con-Tact paper, run a warm iron over it and it should peel right off.
• *Or,* aim a blow dryer at it for several minutes.
• *Instead of* paper, try using floor tiles to line pantry shelves. They clean easily and last forever.

Rust-proofing
• *Store your* current steel scouring pad in a little clay flowerpot. Clay absorbs moisture and helps prevent rusting.
• *Or, wrap* it in foil and stash it in the freezer.

Here's the solution
• *Use old* wine racks to hold cleaning solutions. Just be sure to label the bottle caps and store in a safe place.

Filter action
• *To clean* kitchen drawers without removing the contents, cover your vacuum cleaner nozzle with panty hose or cheesecloth and fasten with a rubber band.

Grate idea

• *When you* have two or more things to grate for one dish, grate the softest one first. Then the firmer foods "clean" the openings in the grater.

• *After grating* cheese, clean the grate by rubbing it with a raw potato.

Put through the grind

• *Before washing* the meat grinder, run a piece of bread through it.

Clean sponges and dishtowels

• *To add* freshness to old sponges, soak them overnight in a bowl of bleach and rinse well in the morning.

• *Or wash* them in the dishwasher.

• *You'll have* a clean towel every day if you wrap your dirty towel around one of the wires on the top shelf of your dishwasher and run it through a cycle.

Taking out the garbage

• *Drop a* twist tie in the bottom of any can or basket before you put the liner in. When you're ready to empty it, the tie is ready.

• *If the* can is deep enough, store extra liners in there as well. There will be a fresh one when you need it.

• *To prevent* paper garbage bags from ripping down the side, turn the top edge of the bag down two inches to form a double edge. Bags won't collapse when you toss them in the garbage.

• *Drive a* stake or broom handle into the ground and slip the side handle of the trash can over it. Can won't tip.

• *Use a* child's skateboard to roll the trash can to the curb on pickup days.

APPLIANCE ADVICE

Blender
• *If it* cannot be taken apart to wash, fill part way with hot water and add a drop of detergent. Cover and turn it on for a few seconds. Rinse and drain dry.
• *To lubricate* blenders, egg beaters, and any other kitchen appliances with movable parts, use mineral oil. Salad oil may corrode the metal. Mineral oil is noncorrosive and, like salad oil, it doesn't harm food.

Coffee pot
• *Clean an* electric coffeepot with Kool-Aid. Run it through entire cycle, then rinse, and dry it thoroughly.

Dishwasher
• *Clean the* inside of your dishwasher by filling the dishwasher cup with Tang (the orange drink) instead of detergent. Wash without dirty dishes and run it through a complete cycle.

Ice maker
• *Automatic ice* maker jammed up because ice cubes have frozen together? Hold a hair-dryer blower about eight inches from the frozen mass until it's melted.

Microwave oven
• *To clean* spills in a microwave oven, cover the spill with a damp paper towel and turn the oven high for

ten seconds. The mess will wipe up easily when the oven cools.

Toasters
• *Shine up* with club soda or a little ammonia and lots of water.
• *Use lighter* fluid or nail-polish remover to remove plastic that has burned on the toaster and any other electrical appliances.

Waffle iron
• *Use a* toothbrush to spread oil around waffle iron. When you're finished using the iron, use the same brush to scrub between the rows with soapy water.

POTS AND PANS

Blackouts
• *Sprinkle burned* pots liberally with baking soda, adding a few cups of water. Simmer on stove a while and then let stand for a few hours. You can usually lift the burned portion right out of the pan.
• *Stubborn black* burn marks: heat pan and spray with oven cleaner. Wait half an hour before scouring.
• *Drop used* fabric-softener pads (the kind you use in your dryer) into cooking utensils caked with baked-on food. Fill with water and let stand for one hour.

Broiler pan
• *Sprinkle the* hot pan heavily with dishwasher detergent or dry laundry detergent. Cover with a damp-

ened paper towel and let the burned food stand for a
while.
• *Or, spray* with oven cleaner.

Cast-iron skillets
• *Boil a* little vinegar and salt in an iron skillet and
watch the black spots and charred food disappear.
• *Clean the* outside of the pan with oven cleaner. Let
it stand for an hour; the accumulated black stains can
then be removed with vinegar and water.
• *After washing* and towel-drying, place the skillet in
a warm oven to complete drying. Moisture is a skillet's worst enemy.
• *Or, when* it's clean, rub a small amount of salad oil
on the inside of the pan to keep it seasoned.
• *If rust* spots appear, apply salad oil and allow to
stand before wiping thoroughly. If rust spots do not
disappear, try the same procedure again.
• *Always place* paper towels between cast-iron pans
when stacking them.
• *If you* have a cast-iron skillet without wooden handles that is encrusted with hard-baked grease on the
outside, clean it by putting the pan in the fireplace.
Let it get red for an hour or so. When it has cooled
off, wash off soot with soapy water, then dry, and oil
it. It'll come out clean as a whistle.

Enamel stains
• *Enamel-pot stains* can be easily removed. When a
dark brown stain develops, mix bleach with water and
boil it in the pot until the stain disappears.

Percolator
• *Fill the* percolator with water, add five tablespoons

of salt, insert the tube, and let perk for fifteen minutes.

• *Restore luster* to a percolator by boiling vinegar in it.

• *Sprinkle some* salt into the strainer and pour hot water over it. This procedure removes the coffee grounds that clog the strainer basket.

• *To clean* the vertical tube of a percolator, run a pipe cleaner through it.

• *To clean* glass coffeepots: Drop in five or six ice cubes and sprinkle with salt. Swish around until the pot is clean.

Stainless and aluminum

• *To make* your stainless-steel pots shine like a mirror, add one-quarter cup of bleach to the bottom of your dishwasher at the beginning of the cycle.

• *To clean* the inside of an aluminum pot that has turned black, boil a solution of two teaspoons of cream of tartar and one quart of water in it for a few minutes.

• *Never use* strong soap or alkaline scouring powders. These products darken and discolor aluminum.

Sticky issues

• *Stubborn stains* on no-stick cookware can be removed by boiling two tablespoons of baking soda, one-half cup of vinegar, and one cup of water in stained pan for fifteen minutes. Reseason pan with salad oil.

Teakettle

• *To remove* lime deposits, fill the kettle with equal

parts of vinegar and water. Bring to a boil and allow to stand overnight.

• *Or, fill* with water and refrigerate for about half a day. The lime is worked free by the cold and will come out when the kettle is emptied.

• *Fill Corningware* teapots with water and drop in two denture-cleaning tablets. Let stand thirty minutes and rinse well.

• *Or, pour* one-quarter cup of vinegar or lemon juice in the pot and fill with hot water. Let stand a couple of hours, then rinse.

IMPROVISE, DON'T AGONIZE

Cheesecloth Strainer
• *A clean* section of pantyhose will do.

Coffee Filter
• *Use a* piece of paper toweling.

Cutting board
• *For a* good cutting board that can be taken anywhere, cover a thick magazine or several layers of cardboard with heavy duty aluminum foil.

Flour Duster
• *Keep a* powder puff in your flour container. It's excellent for dusting flour on rolling pins, pastry boards, and other surfaces.

Funnel
• *Make an* instant funnel for dry substances such as

sugar, salt, or flour by clipping the corner from an envelope or paper bag.

• *For liquids:* Clip the corners from a plastic bag or the fingertip of a rubber glove.

• *Or use* a gravy boat.

• *Or cut* a detergent bottle in half and clean it thoroughly.

Hot Pad

• *Use the* magazine or cardboard covered with aluminum foil.

• *Or use* a place mat.

• *Or use* a pot holder. Under the hot dish, it won't be seen.

Measuring Cup

• *Use an* ice-cream scoop: the average one holds exactly one-third cup.

Oyster and clam opener

• *Use a* beer can opener to open oysters. Insert the point under the hinge at the top of the oyster and push down hard.

Rack or counter space

• *Slide out* a refrigerator shelf and use it as a cooling rack if you're baking a lot of cakes or bread.

• *Or cool* a pie or cake on a gas burner grate.

• *Create extra* counter space when doing a lot of baking. Pull out a drawer or two and place a cookie sheet or tray across the top.

Rolling pin

• *Use a* wine bottle, filled with cold water and recorked, as a quick and efficient rolling pin.

• *Or use* a cold bottle of soda pop wrapped in a stocking.

Steamer
• *If you* don't have a steamer, improvise. Set a round strainer into a pan deep enough to hold several inches of water. The water level should be just below the strainer so that it doesn't touch or boil into it. You're ready to steam.

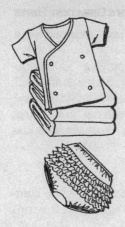

17

Best of Helpful Hints for Laundry

GET READY, GET SET

Cleaning your machine
• *Fill the* washer with warm water and pour a gallon of distilled vinegar into it. Run the machine through an entire cycle. The vinegar will cleanse the hoses and unclog soap scum from them.

Sock it to them
• *Set a* small wastebasket in each child's room and tell them to use it as a mini-hamper for soiled socks.
• *Save yourself* the trouble of sorting dark socks. Make a small laundry bag for each family member, using dish towels or mesh fabric with a drawstring top. Personalize the bags by making each a different color. Toss the bags into the washer and when they come out of the dryer, the socks are already sorted.

Stain reminder
• *Tie a* knot in a sleeve or pant leg to remind you that it needs special washing care.

Prewash treatments
• *Remove spots* cheaply by applying automatic-dishwasher detergent to wet fabric. Scrub gently with an old toothbrush. Rinse.
• *Before washing* a garment with a drawstring, safety-pin the string to the clothing. Now you can toss it safely into the washer.

Fringe
• *Keep long-tasseled* fringe from tangling while laundering by tying every six strands together at the tops with string to make one large tassel.

WASHDAY WISDOM

The best way to clean whites
• *Pour one* gallon of hot water into a plastic container and add one-half cup of automatic-dishwasher soap and one-half cup of bleach. Mix well. Soak clothing overnight in this mixture, then, in the morning, dump solution and clothes into the washing machine and wash as usual. Add one-half cup of white vinegar to the rinse water. (If you use this formula on nylon or synthetics, allow the water to cool a bit, as hot water sets wrinkles.)
• *To whiten* old or dull white polyester, soak it overnight in a bucket filled with one gallon of water and one cup of automatic-dishwater detergent. In the morning, toss the polyester into the machine and wash as usual. Use this on uniforms that are no longer white.

Make your own fabric softener sheets
• *Pour a* few capfuls of any fabric softener into a small bowl of water. Swish a washcloth or an old sock in the solution. Wring it out and toss into the dryer along with the wet clothes. It's that simple. But best of all, it's a lot less expensive than using the tear-off sheet brands.

Old softies
• *After fabric-softener* sheets have been used twice, store them in a jar with some liquid fabric softener. When drying a load of clothes, just squeeze out the excess liquid from one of the sheets and toss it in the dryer.

Machine washing dainty garments
• *Drop your* dainty garments into a pillowcase and fasten the loose end with a plastic bag tie. Place in washer and wash on a gentle cycle.

Too many suds
• *Any time* your washing machine overflows from too many suds, pour in a little fabric softener. Suds will disappear.

RINSE SENSE

Make it thorough
• *To make* sure clothes receive a thorough rinsing, add one cup of white vinegar to the rinse cycle. This will help dissolve the alkalines in soaps and deter-

gents. Plus, it will give you soft and sweet-smelling clothing for just pennies.

• *The vinegar* is a must for hand washing. It cuts down soap so fast you will only have to rinse two times.

Sweet notion

• *Add a* sprinkling of your favorite bath salts to the last rinse water when washing blankets, robes, and spreads. Let fabric soak for about ten minutes and it comes out sweet-smelling.

Plastic softener

• *Keep plastic* items such as shower curtains or baby pants soft and pliable. Add a few ounces of glycerin when rinsing them.

Creme rinse your sweaters

• *For the* best results when hand washing sweaters, put a capful of creme rinse in the final rinse water.

• *Or, rinse* wool garments in lukewarm water and a few tablespoons of glycerin. This will keep them soft and will also help prevent itching when they are worn.

HOLD THAT LINE

Dealing with your hangups

• *Large shag* rugs: Hang them wrong side out, so the tufted surfaces will rub against each other and raise the pile.

• *Sheets: Hang* them over two parallel clotheslines. They'll dry faster and flap less, too, and you'll save wear and tear on the fiber.

Pot luck

• A *plastic* hanging plant pot makes a great weather-proof clothespin holder for the clothesline. When it rains, the water will drain out of the holes in the planter's bottom.

This trick's self-taut

• *Does your* clothesline sag? Put a link chain at one end, and instead of having to bother with re-tying, just move the chain up one or two links.

Anti-freeze

• *A handful* of salt in the wash day rinse water will keep clothes from sticking or freezing to the clothes-line on damp, cold days.

DRIED AND TRUE

Faster drying of hand washables

• *Throw a* clean bath towel into the dryer with the clothes. The towel absorbs moisture and clothes will dry faster.

Buttoned up

• *Before putting* clothes into the dryer, turn them inside out and button them. The buttons won't be damaged by banging against the sides of the dryer.

Clang control

• *To keep* overall buckles from clanging in the dryer, put each buckle into one of the back pockets and pin in place.

Taking the wrinkles out
• *New spreads,* tablecloths, and drapes: Put them in the dryer with a large, damp towel. Set the dryer on "warm" and let them tumble for about ten minutes.
• *New plastic* shower curtains and plastic cloths: Toss in the dryer with a large damp towel, but set the dial for "air fluff."

PRESSING SITUATIONS

A fast way to dampen clothes
• *Place clothes* in dryer and add two thoroughly wet bath towels. Set dryer on a "no-heat" setting and let clothing tumble until desired dampness is arrived at.

Take a break
• *If you* have dampened ironing that you can't finish, stick it in the refrigerator or freezer until you are ready to catch up. It won't mildew and will be ready to iron when you are.

Stop the presses
• *Remove blouses* from the dryer while still wet. Hang them on hangers, smooth out at the buttons, and spray with starch. Let dry and pressing is eliminated.

Easy starching
• *If you've* got a lot of laundry that needs starching, spray the starch while it's wet and hanging on the line. This way, you can spray from both sides. It's ready to iron.

• *If you* like collar, cuffs, and button bands extra stiff, fill an empty, clean roll-on deodorant bottle with liquid starch and apply the desired amount. (To remove the roll-on ball from the bottle, gently pry the top off with a nail file.)

Faster ironing
• *For smoother* ironing, frequently run your warm iron over waxed paper. Be sure to run the iron over a clean cloth or a paper towel before ironing again.

Creaseless sleeves
• *To press* a jacket or dress sleeve without making a crease, roll up a thick magazine, cover it with a cloth, and insert it in the sleeve. The magazine immediately unrolls enough to make a firm pressing pad.

Ironing embroidery
• *Lay the* embroidery piece upside down on a turkish towel before ironing. All the little spaces between the embroidery will be smooth when you are finished.

GET IT STRAIGHT

Pressing pleats
• *When pleats* are pressed, the folds sometimes leave marks on the pleats above. Avoid this by placing long strips of brown paper under each pleat.

Sharp pant creases
• *Use a* dampened brown grocery bag (with no lettering) for pressing sharp creases. It's especially good

for pressing seams on tailored garments.

• *For a* sharp, permanent crease in slacks, steam-iron them as usual, then turn slacks inside out and run a candle along the crease. Turn pants right side out and steam-iron them again. This method is great for wash-and-wear fabric.

Unwrinkled sheers

• *If pressing* doesn't get sheer curtains to hang straight, slip a curtain rod through the bottom hem and let them hang for a few days. When rods are removed, curtains will fall right.

TOOLS OF THE TRADE

To clean starch stickiness off irons

• *Run the* iron across a piece of aluminum foil or paper sprinkled with salt. (*Not* for Teflon-coated irons.)

• *Or, remove* the stickiness with a little rubbing alcohol.

• *Or, try* heating the iron, then run it over a soft, small rag. When the iron's cooled, make a paste of mild scouring powder and a little water to remove any remaining residue.

• *Or, if* starch sticks to the soleplate or bottom of the iron, let the iron cool and apply paste silver polish. Then wipe with a damp cloth and dry.

Ironing board cover

• *Repair worn* spots and tears on your ironing board: cover with iron-on patches.

• *If your* cover needs laundering, remember it will fit tightly and smoothly after washing if you fasten it on the board while it's still damp.

SORTING IT OUT

Cutting down on sorting time
• *Hang clothes* to be ironed on the line first and follow with clothes that need only to be folded.

To each his jeans
• *Can't tell* those jeans apart when sorting the laundry? Use laundry marking pens and place each child's first initial on the inside pocket.

Sheet strategies
• *When buying* sheets for different beds, choose different colors for each one and you'll always know which sheets go where.

A new wrinkle
• *Store seldom-used* linens by folding them wrong side out. Dust won't show on the crease lines.

Putting clothes away
• *If you* could use more help sorting and returning clean clothes to their owners, put up a shelf in the laundry room. Set plastic dishpans on it and label each pan with a family member's name. On washday each person can collect his own clothing.

Do it yourself
• *Get each* family member a different color laundry

basket and they can be responsible for sorting and putting their laundry away.

• *Put up* a floor-to-ceiling plant pole in your laundry room to hang freshly dried clothes. Let everyone retrieve his own clothing.

THE TOPIC IS LINT

No more lint

• *You will* eliminate the lint problem by adding one cup of white vinegar to the final rinse cycle.

• *Or, put* a yard of nylon netting into the dryer with wet clothes to act as a lint catcher.

• *Keep a* plastic mesh pot scrubber near the dryer. When trap needs to be cleaned, one quick swipe with the scrubber does the trick.

To get rid of excess lint on new chenille

• *Tumble-dry dry* chenille spreads, draperies, or throw rugs for about five to ten minutes.

Lint removers

• *To remove* lint from corduroy, wash and allow to dry very slowly. While clothing is still damp brush with a clothes brush. All the lint will come off, but remember—the clothing must be damp.

• *Use a* pom-pom made of nylon net to remove lint quickly from clothes while ironing. Brush the net ball over the clothes and the lint will disappear. For handy usage, attach the net to the ironing board with string.

• *Or use* a large synthetic sponge to take lint off synthetic clothing. This works especially well on polyester double-knits, which seem to attract lint in the wash.

Lint regulations
• *If the* lint under and around the filter of the dryer seems damp, it means the outside vent is clogged. You'd better clean it out before the machine breaks down.
• *To keep* lint from clogging your drain, secure an old nylon stocking over your washing-machine hose with a heavy-duty rubber band.
• *Or, cut* a piece of window screening big enough to cover the bottom of the sink. To remove lint from the screen, simply scrub with a damp brush.

REVIVAL TECHNIQUES

Cleaning velvet
• *The best* velvet brush is another small piece of velvet rubbed down the nap of the garment.

Press on
• *Revive velvet* or corduroy by pressing it facedown on a piece of the same fabric.

Renovating stiffened chamois
• *Soak in* warm water to which a spoonful or so of olive oil has been added.

Cleaning black lace
• *Dip a* sponge into cold tea and just dampen the lace, don't soak. Put a piece of brown paper over it and press with a warm iron.

Shrunken woolen item
• *Soak in* tepid water to which you have added a good hair shampoo. Sometimes this will soften the wool fibers enough to allow for a reshaping. It's worth a try.

Renovating feather pillows
• *Set dryer* on "air" setting and let pillows tumble for fifteen minutes. However, make sure there are no holes in the pillow or the feathers will work through.

Wrinkled, "overdried" permanent press items
• *Set the* dryer for ten minutes and toss in a wet towel.

WHEN STAINS ARE A PAIN

Baby stains
• *Get rid* of baby-food stains with this solution: one cup of bleach, one cup of dishwater detergent, and two to three gallons of water. Let material soak a few hours before washing it.
• *To remove* odor instantly from spit-ups, apply a paste of baking soda and water to the fabric.

Ballpoint ink
• *Apply hairspray* liberally to stain. Rub with a clean, dry cloth and the ink usually disappears. This works exceptionally well on polyester fabrics.
• *Or, try* rubbing alcohol on the spot before laundering.

Blood
• *Cover area* with meat tenderizer. Apply cool water to make a paste. Wait fifteen to thirty minutes, sponge with cool water.
• *Hydrogen peroxide* will take out a fresh stain.

Candle wax or crayon
• *Place the* stained area between clean paper towels or pieces of a brown paper bag. Press with warm iron.

Fruit stains
• *Remove stain* by stretching the stained area over a bowl and pouring boiling water, from a height of several feet, through the stain.

Grease
• *Along with* detergent, add a bottle of Coke to a load of greasy work clothes. It will help loosen serious grease stains.

Makeup
• *A slice* of bread will often remove makeup smudges from dark clothes.

Ring around the collar
• *Use a* small paintbrush and brush hair shampoo into soiled shirt collars before laundering. Shampoo is made to dissolve body oils.
• *Mark heavily* with chalk. The chalk will absorb the oils and once the oil is removed, the dirt will come off easily. This method may require a few applications if the yellow line has been there for some time. If the shirt is new, one application should do it.
• *Or, apply* a paste of vinegar and baking soda. Rub

in and wash as usual. This method also removes dirt and mildew.

Rust
• *Apply lemon* juice and salt, then place in the sun.
• *Rust can* also be removed from white washables by covering the stains with cream of tartar, then gathering up the ends of the article so that the powder stays on the spot. Dip the entire spot into hot water for about five minutes. Ordinary laundering will complete the job.

Scorch
• *On whites,* sponge with a piece of cotton which has been soaked in peroxide. Use the three-percent solution sold as a mild antiseptic.
• *For linen* and cotton, dampen a cloth with peroxide, lay it on the scorched area, and iron with a warm iron.

Shoe polish
• *Remove with* rubbing alcohol. Use one part alcohol and two parts water on colored fabric. Use it straight on whites.

Tar
• *Rub the* tar spot with kerosene until removed, then wash with detergent and water. The kerosene will not take the color out of most fabrics—but you'd better test it first.

Wine
• *Sprinkle the* spill immediately with lots of salt. Dunk into cold water and rub the stain out before washing.

DYE IDEAS

Colorfasting

• *When setting* the dye in clothing, always do each article separately. Add one-half cup of vinegar and one tablespoon of salt to one-half gallon of water. Soak fabric for one hour. If rinse water still shows some color, repeat.

• *A teaspoon* of Epsom salts to one gallon of rinse water will help keep most materials from fading or running.

When colors bleed

• *Rit Color* Remover (sold where dyes are) is meant to remove this kind of problem.

Hints for tints

• *Help disperse* dye thoroughly by adding water softener to the dye or tint bath. Unless directions call for straining, this tip will work.

• *Tie the* dye powder in a piece of lightweight cloth, then pour boiling water over it until all the dye is dissolved. This should eliminate the problem of clumped-together, undissolved dye particles that can spot what you're dyeing.

18

Best of Helpful Hints for Miscellaneous Cleaning Jobs

Artificial flowers

• *Pour some* salt into a large paper bag with the flowers. Shake vigorously. The salt won't look soiled, but wait until you see its color when you run water on it.

Ashtrays

• *Ashtrays* (not glass ones!) will be easier to clean if polished with furniture polish.

Brass

• *Apply a* thin coat of window cleaner with a soft cloth, let dry and rub lightly with polish. Brass will be tarnish free for months.

• *Mix equal* parts of salt and flour and add a little vinegar to make a paste. Spread a thick layer on the brass and let it dry. Rinse and wipe off paste.

• *Or, use* toothpaste or very fine steel wool dipped in furniture polish.

266

Candles

• *Sponge with* a piece of cotton dampened with rubbing alcohol.

Candle holders

• *If your* candleholders are coated with wax, place in the freezer for an hour or so. The wax will peel off in a jiffy with absolutely no injury to the silver.

• *Or, run* under very hot water and dry with a paper towel.

Chandeliers

• *Here is* a method of cleaning crystal chandeliers that does not require disassembling the fixture. The area underneath the chandelier should be protected by a drop cloth. Fill a water tumbler with one part alcohol to three parts water. Raise the tumbler to each pendant until it is immersed. The crystal will drip dry without leaving water spots, lint, or finger marks. The crystal parts not accessible to the tumbler can be wiped with the solution.

• *Or, wear* cotton work gloves and dip your fingers in ammonia water and clean away.

Ceiling

• *Wrap cloth* around your broom head and secure it with a rubber band, then sweep away dust and cobwebs.

Cigarette smoke

• *Soak a* towel in water, wring it out thoroughly, and swish it around the room. Smoke will disappear quickly.

• *Put small* bowls of vinegar in four corners of the room where smokers are congregating.

• *Or, place* activated charcoal in small dishes to remove post-party odors.

• *Also, burn* candles to eliminate the smoke.

Copper
• *Fill a* spray bottle with hot vinegar and add three tablespoons of salt. Spray solution liberally on copper pots. Let sit for a while, then rub it clean.

• *Or, try* lemon juice and salt.

Door
• *Is your* child sticker-crazy? Hang a large sheet of clear plastic adhesive-backed paper on the door or wall before he puts any up. Stickers just peel right off when he tires of them.

Dusting
• *To get* at dust on louvered doors, wrap a cloth around a ruler, spray with your favorite dusting spray, and run the flat end across each louver.

• *Use a* child's dust mop for dusting hard-to-reach places such as above doors, paneled walls, etc.

• *Or, put* an old sock over a yardstick and secure with a rubber band. This also comes in handy for cleaning cobwebs off the ceiling.

• *A four-inch* paintbrush is good for dusting lamp shade pleats, windowsills, etc.

• *Spray some* furniture polish on the bristles of your broom and the dust and dirt will be easier to collect when you sweep.

• *Cut down* on the dust circulating through your home by spraying the furnace filter with Endust.

• *Or, cut* used fabric-softener sheets or pieces of nylon to fit your floor registers. Slip them under the vent as air filters.

Fireplaces

• *There is* less need to scrub the fireplace if you throw salt on the logs occasionally. This will reduce the soot by two-thirds.

• *Vinegar will* clean brick tiling around the fireplace. Dip a vegetable brush in white vinegar and scrub quickly. Sponge immediately to absorb the moisture.

• *Rub smoked* areas with an art gum eraser. This works especially well on porous, rock-front fireplaces.

• *For smooth* stone or brick fireplaces, wash with a strong solution of trisodium phosphate (one-half cup to one gallon of water). Apply with sponge. Use this solution only after all the smoke possible has been erased with an art-gum eraser.

• *For big* jobs: Add four ounces of naptha soap to one quart of hot water. Heat until soap dissolves. Cool, then stir in one-half pound of powdered pumice and one-half cup of household ammonia. Mix thoroughly. Remove as much of the smoky deposit as you can before applying a coat of the soap mixture with a paintbrush. Allow it to remain on for thirty minutes. Scrub with a scrub brush and warm water. Sponge with plenty of water to rinse.

• *Clean the* smoke film from glass fireplace doors by rubbing on fireplace ashes with a damp cloth. Buff with another damp cloth and the glass will come clean.

• *To prevent* soot from settling all over the house, dampen fireplace ashes with a plant mister before cleaning them out. Then shovel ashes into a box and cover it with wet newspapers.

• *Run a* candle stub along the track of your fireplace screen to keep it sliding easily.

Frames
• *Wipe with* a soft sponge moistened with turpentine. If the gilt seems a bit sticky after you finish, let dry for a day or two without touching.

Golf balls
• *Soak them* in one cup of water and one-quarter cup of ammonia.

Golf clubs
• *Rub the* shaft and club heads lightly with a dry steel wool sponge.

Guitar
• *Rub toothpaste* on your guitar, let it dry, then buff for a super shine.

Knickknacks
• *Don't dust* each knickknack individually. Collect them in a dishpan and bathe them in a little detergent and water. Rinse and dry them with a hair dryer.
• *For delicate* figurines that can't be washed, use artist's red-sable paintbrush #2 or #4. The long handle lets you get to hard-to-reach places and the little brush allows you to dust without breaking the object.

Marble
• *Try covering* the stained area with three percent hydrogen peroxide. Let it set for several hours and wipe up with a dampened cloth. Marble stains are difficult to remove but this hint is worth a try.

Mattresses
• *Use an* upholstery shampoo to remove mattress

stains. Spray the area with disinfectant air freshener to prevent mustiness.

Odors: Nothing to sniff about

• *Make the* whole house fresher. Put a solid room deodorizer next to the return vent of your forced-air heating system.

• *To eliminate* odors in home humidifiers, pour three or four capfuls of bottled lemon juice in the water.

• *Lighted candles* will help keep rooms free of cigarette smoke.

• *Eliminate odors* and have a fresh-smelling house for just pennies by putting a few drops of wintergreen oil (available at drugstores) on a cotton ball and placing it in a glass container. It will last for months and is as effective as room sprays.

• *Toss dried* orange and lemon rinds into your fireplace for a spicy aroma.

High-gloss paneling

• *Add one* cup of any type of time-saving floor wax to one gallon of water. Wash with a soft cloth. This solution helps guard against finger marks, too.

Pewter

• *To clean old* pewter, use a mild kitchen scouring powder moistened with olive oil. For a very stubborn stain, dip very fine steel wool in water or kerosene and rub gently. Rinse with soap and water.

• *Today's new* pewter requires a minimum of cleaning because it is made from a tarnish-proof alloy. It can be cleaned by washing with soap and water.

• *Or, try* a homemade mixture of wood ashes moistened with water on both new and old pewter.

Pictures
• *Use some* eyeglass-cleaning tissues (instead of a wet cloth) to clean the glass on a small picture; no water can seep under the glass or damage the frame.
• *Dust oil* paintings every few months with a soft brush. Never rub the painting with a cloth.

Plastic
• *Try using* a rag dampened with lemon oil to prevent smears.

Playing cards
• *Clean plastic* playing cards by dropping the deck into a paper bag and adding a few tablespoons of flour. Shake briskly, then wipe completely clean.

Pleated lamp shades
• *Blow dust* away with a hand-held hair dryer.
• *Or use* an old shaving brush.
• *Or try* a paintbrush.

Radiators
• *Place a* wet towel under the radiator and vacuum excess dust from fins. Blowing down through the fins with the blower end of the vacuum gets rid of even more dust. The wet towel beneath the register collects the excess.

Sliding door tracks
• *Generally, the* tracks of sliding glass doors are very hard to clean. Try wrapping a small cloth around an eraser and rub dirt away.

Steam irons
• *To remove* mineral deposits from the inside of a

steam iron, fill it with equal parts of water and white vinegar. Let it steam for several minutes, then disconnect, and let set for one hour. Empty and rinse out with clear water.

• *Remove brown* or burned-on spots by rubbing with a heated solution of vinegar and salt.

• *Remove wax* buildup by rubbing with very fine sandpaper. Next, polish with a piece of fine soapless steel wool, then wipe off with a damp cloth.

• *Or, clean* the outside of your iron with toothpaste or silver polish.

Telephone

• *Clean your* telephone with rubbing alcohol to keep it new-looking.

Vases with small openings

• *Dampen the* inside of the vase and add any toilet bowl cleaner. Let stand for ten minutes and stains will disappear.

• *Or, fill* with hot water and add two tablespoons of vinegar plus some rice and shake well.

Vacuuming

• *Put petroleum* jelly on the ends of the vacuum cleaner extension wands and they'll slide apart easily.

• *Prevent a* retractable vacuum cleaner cord from snapping back into the machine when you don't want it to. Pull the cord out as far as you want, then attach a spring-type clothespin to it. Adjust as needed.

• *No need* to replace your fabric vacuum-cleaner bag when it tears. Simply mend it by pressing iron-on patches over the hole.

Walls

• *Homemade wall* cleaner: One-half cup of ammonia,

one-quarter cup of white vinegar, one-fourth cup of washing soda and one gallon of warm water.

• *Always begin* washing walls at the bottom instead of the top and wash upward. If dirty water runs down over soiled areas, it leaves streaks that are harder to remove.

• *To remove* everyday smudges, erase light marks with gum eraser (from stationery and art supply stores).

• *Or rub* the soiled areas with chunks of fresh bread.

• *For grease,* sprinkle white talcum powder on a clean powder puff. Rub the puff over the spot, repeating the process until the grease disappears.

• *Or make* a paste of cornstarch or fuller's earth and water. Let it remain on the spot for a few hours, then brush it off. If the stain is still present, try again.

19

Best of
Helpful Hints
for Outdoors

FOR GOOD SPORTS

Smooth sledding
• *A child's* sled will go down the hill faster if you spray vegetable oil on the bottom. Works on inner tubes, too.

Net profit
• *Have your* tennis balls lost their bounce? If so, place the can of balls with the lid off overnight in a closed oven. The heat from the pilot light will get them back into shape.

In the swing
• *Slit sections* of discarded rubber hose and, with super-hold glue, attach them to the edges of your youngsters' swing seats. The hose acts as a bumper if the swing accidentally hits one of the kids.
• *Cover swing* chains with garden hose for a steadier grip.

At the beach with baby
• *A big* sheet will be cooler than a blanket for you and baby to sit on. It shakes clean more easily, too.
• *Fill a* mesh bag with beach toys. It can all be dunked in the water to clean and drain dry.

HAVE A PICNIC

Thermos be a way to solve this
• *For a* shrunken Thermos cork, boil the cork in a covered pot until it expands to fill the bottle again.
• *To prevent* the cork from souring in a Thermos, place a small piece of plastic wrap over the cork.

Blow-away insurance
• *To prevent* picnic tablecloths from blowing in the wind, put two-sided adhesive tape here and there on the table, especially in the corners.
• *Or, try* a fitted sheet for a junior-sized bed. Most are the same size as a standard picnic table and fit the tabletop as they do a bed.

Cool ideas
• *Melted paraffin* wax applied to the inside and outside of a cooler leak will seal it.
• *Use a* sugar bag instead of a plastic bag for storing ice cubes because it's thicker and insulates better.

No butts about it
• *Keep a* few flowerpots filled with sand near smokers and stop worrying that they will litter the grass.

IN THE YARD

Make your own outdoor drinking fountain
• *Install a* faucet—upside down.
• *For fast* cleanups from your outside faucet, hang a bar of soap in an onion net bag on it. Wash your hands without even taking the soap out of the bag.

Good awning
• *Make old* canvas look like new by painting with canvas paint (available at paint stores.)
• *Eliminate bird* droppings with a stiff brush that has been run over a bar of naphtha soap and sprinkled with dry washing soda. Hose well to rinse.

GRILL WORK

Marination sensations
• *To marinate* meats easily, place in a plastic bag with sauce and seal tightly. Turning the bag just once coats all the pieces at the same time.
• *To tenderize* chicken or pork chops, boil them in a saucepan for fifteen minutes. Then drain and let marinate in barbecue sauce for thirty minutes. Now meat is ready to barbecue.

In the can
• *A sure* way to start a charcoal fire: punch a few holes in the sides of a coffee can, remove both ends, and set it in the grill. Fill with charcoal, add starter fluid, and light. When the coals are glowing, remove

the can with tongs and set it in a safe place. Spread
the coals and replace the grill.

Light your fire
• *Pour enough* briquettes for one barbecue into a grocery bag and fold it down. When you have a quantity
of bags filled, pile one on top of the other until ready
to barbecue. Then simply place one paper bag of briquettes in the barbecue and light. The charcoal will
catch very quickly and you will have clean hands.
• *Pack charcoal* briquettes in egg cartons and tie
shut. There's no mess and you can light them right in
the carton in the barbecue.

Is it ready?
• *You'll know* if the outdoor grill is ready to start
cooking if you use this easy test. Hold your hand over
the grill at the approximate level the food will be
cooked at—and be careful. If you can only hold your
hand there to the count of three, the fire is hot. If you
get to a count of five, the fire is at medium and a
count of eight means the fire is low.

Fire tending
• *To prevent* burns when roasting hot dogs and
marshmallows on a stick, cut a hole in the center of
an old pie tin and slip the stick through it. The pie tin
shields the hand.
• *Or, for* other work near the fire, a canvas work
glove soaked in water protects the hands. *Note*:
Never touch extremely hot objects with wet gloves.

Fast action for flare-ups
• *When flare-ups* from fat drippings start to burn the
meat, place lettuce leaves over the hot coals.

• *Or, keep* a pan of water and a turkey baster next to the barbecue, and squirt water to put out flare-ups.
• *Or, when* flare-ups occur, simply place the coals farther apart and raise the grill.

Cool it down
• *You can* cool down the fire without extinguishing it if you sprinkle water over it with a clean whisk broom.

Thinking ahead
• *Coat the* bottoms of pots and pans with shaving cream or bar soap before cooking on open fire. The black marks come off without much scouring.
• *Coat the* grill with vegetable oil before cooking. Begin cleaning as soon as the grill is cool to the touch.

On the spot
• *Wipe the* grill with a piece of crumpled aluminum foil while it's still warm.
• *Or, spray* a greasy grill while it's still warm with a window cleaner.
• *Or, using* a thick kitchen mitt, wrap the grill in several layers of wet newspaper while it's still hot. It steams itself clean.

Afterthoughts
• *When the* grill is cool, place it inside a plastic garbage bag and add enough powdered dishwater detergent and hot water to cover the grill. Tie the bag shut and let it sit outside for a few hours. Rinse it completely before using it again.
• *File a* notch in the blunt end of a beer can opener and use it to scrape a cold, blackened grill.

LET'S GO CAMPING

Fast ways to do laundry
• *On camping* trips, use a clean plunger as an agitator and a plastic bucket as a washtub when doing small laundry jobs.
• *Or put* dirty clothes, detergent, and water in a large container with a tight-fitting lid. Set it in your car trunk, and while you're driving to the next campsite, the dirty clothes will be swishing around and cleaning themselves.

Bright ideas for flashlights
• *Put a* piece of tape over the flashlight switch so it won't get turned on accidentally in the suitcase.
• *Protect your* flashlight in the rain. Put it in a plastic sandwich bag and close the opening with a rubber band. You can turn it on and off without removing it, and the light will shine brightly through the plastic.

Matches
• *Wrap kitchen* matches in aluminum foil to keep them dry on fishing, camping, and other outdoor trips.

Ice chests
• *Pre-chill the* interior by filling the chest with ice. Let it stand for at least fifteen minutes, then drain, and cover the bottom with plenty of fresh ice cubes.
• *Or, if* you've got the space, put the chest directly into the freezer.

To hang a roll of paper towels outside.
• *It's a* cinch when you use a wire hanger that's got a

narrow paper tube bottom bar. Just pull the wire out of one end of the paper tube, insert the roll of toweling, then push the wire back in the tube.

Mini ovens
• *Roast potatoes* over an open fire, but drop them into an empty tin can so they won't char.

Cleaning cast-iron without water
• *First wipe* out the pan with a paper towel. Pour a tablespoon or two of salt into the skillet, then scrub the pan clean with another paper towel. Salt will absorb grease while acting like scouring powder. Wipe out remaining salt.

Grit-free soap
• *Slip a* bar of soap into a nylon stocking to prevent any sand from getting on the soap when bathing in a lake.

Substitute clotheslines
• *Fold a* long rope in half and wrap the middle of it around a tree. Hold the two ends together and twist them around a tree. Tie the ends to another tree. To hang clothes, just slip a piece of them between the double twisted rope. You won't need pins.
• *Or, try* an old pair of panty hose. The nylon stretches to about 2.7 yards.

Just whistle an SOS
• *Carry along* a whistle when you head for the woods. If you should become lost, blow it sharply three times and repeat this pattern every few minutes. Any kind of signal repeated three times at frequent intervals is a universal call and should bring help.

GONE FISHING

• *Keep your* fishing license in an old ballpoint pen. Remove the cartridge, roll up the license, and stuff it inside the pen. Toss in your tackle box or clip it to your shirt pocket.

• *Ever try* to pull a worm from the bottom of the can? Take a can with a plastic top and cut out both ends. Put plastic covers on each. When you want a worm, open up the end where it is.

• *Wrap a* triple thickness of aluminum foil around the hook immediately after taking the rod out of the water. The hook won't stick anybody or get tangled up with other rods in the boats.

20

Best of Helpful Hints for Pets and Pests

WHEN A PET HAS AN ACCIDENT

Spot sends regrets
• *Blot up* as much moisture as possible. Rub with a solution of vinegar or lemon juice and warm sudsy water. Blot and blot some more. Then pour straight club soda over the spot. Blot again. Place a dry towel over the stain and put a heavy book on top of it. If the towel becomes soggy, immediately replace with a clean, dry one.

Puff made a mess
• *Follow the* above procedure, but once the spot has dried, rub with a cloth dampened in ammonia. This will not only take the offensive odor away, but it will prevent the cat from ever doing it again in the same spot.

On the go
• *Or, to* get rid of odors from pet accidents, first blot the area with paper towels, getting up as much of the

283

mess as possible. Then shampoo the kitchen carpet or mop the floor with a strong solution of Massengill douche liquid. Carpets may need a few applications.

WASHING UP

Rub-a-dub-dub

• *A creme* rinse is helpful for dogs whose fur tangles when wet.

• *Fill a* tub with warm water and put a rubber mat on the bottom for secure footing.

• *Put cotton* in your dog's ears to keep out water and a little petroleum jelly around his eyes to protect them from soap.

• *Add a* little baking soda, vinegar, or lemon juice to the rinse water to make your pet's coat softer, shinier, and odor-free.

Hair catcher

• *If your* pet is shedding, place a tea strainer in the tub drain to keep pipes from clogging up.

Dry cleaning your pet

• *Instead of* always giving your dog a regular bath, rub baking soda into his coat thoroughly and then brush it off. It deodorizes as well as cleans.

• *Dry cornmeal* is also a good dry shampoo for any furry pet. Rub it in well, then brush it out.

If the skunk got Fido

• *In a* well-ventilated area, wash the pet down with tomato juice before washing thoroughly with shampoo and water. Rinse with a gallon of water to which a few

tablespoons of ammonia have been added. Rinse the
pet thoroughly with clear water.

• *Another good* solution is equal parts of vinegar and
water. Wash thoroughly and rinse with clear water,
followed by another good dousing of the vinegar-and-
water solution. However, for this rinse, make it
weaker.

Removing burrs

• *Remove burrs* by working oil into the tangle or by
crushing the burrs with pliers. Crushed burrs lose
their holding power and can be combed out.

CHOW TIME

Hold it

• *Your pet's* dish won't slide across the floor while he
eats if it's set on a rubber mat.
• *Or glue* a rubber jar ring to the bottom of his bowl.

Water bearer

• *Your dog* has the habit of knocking over his water
dish? Set an angel-food cake pan over a wooden stake
driven into the ground.

"Canned" dog food

• *Store big* bags of dry dog food in a clean garbage
can with a lid.

Let 'em eat fishcakes

• *Your cat* will eat only the food from the expensive
small cans? Try mixing in a little of the less-expensive

food that comes in the larger cans. Increase the amount of the cheaper brand in each day's mixture, until the cat will eat it without turning up his tail.
• *Or*, *spill* some oil from a can of tuna over his food.

A HEALTHY ANIMAL

Giving your dog a pill
• *Most dogs* love chocolate candy, so if yours refuses to swallow a pill, push the tablet into a piece of candy. You could also hide the pill in a chunk of dog food.

A safety tip for Rover
• *Tape reflector* tape on your dog's or cat's collar to help cut down the danger of its being struck by a car at night.

Cat Rx
• *When your* cat refuses liquid medicine, spill some on his fur, on an area he can easily reach with his tongue. He'll instinctively lick it off.

TRAINING PROCEDURES

Puppy love
• *When caring* for a litter of puppies or kittens, place them in an old mesh playpen. For pens with wooden slats, tape fine screen around the pen so they don't fall out.

• *Put some* of your old clothes in the puppy's box so he'll pick up your scent and be comforted by it.

Chewing puppy

• *If your* new puppy is chewing on your table and chair legs, solve the problem by putting a little oil of cloves (available at drug departments) on the wood with a piece of cotton. If the odor does not keep him away, the bitter taste will.

Keeping the cat off your favorite chair

• *Stuff a* few mothballs in the cushion of a chair or sofa and your cat will stay off it.
• *Cats also* hate the smell of chili sauce. If your cat is climbing and scratching woodwork, just rub the area with chili sauce, buff off thoroughly, and your cat will stay away. Use this hint only for dark woodwork.
• *And, cats* hate plastic coverings! Cover your chair until your cat realizes the chair is a no-no.

DOG STORIES

Portable dog anchor

• *Make a* portable dog anchor by tying his leash around an old tire and putting a few bricks inside.

In the doghouse

• *Make an* entrance flap for a doghouse out of a piece of indoor/outdoor carpeting. Cut it to size, slit it up the middle, and nail it into place.
• *Or use* a rubber floor mat. Guide your dog through the flap a few times until he learns how to do it himself.

Let sleeping dogs lie

• *If your* dog sleeps under your bed, save the time and trouble of removing hair from the box springs by fitting an old contour sheet to the underside. Just wash it when it gets dirty. This is a good idea even if you don't have a pet.

CAT TALES

Play time

• *Cats love* scratching sounds. Crumple a piece of aluminum foil into a ball and let your kitten bat it around on a hard surface.

• *Or suspend* a ping-pong ball on a piece of string from an empty shelf. Cats love to jump up and hit things, and the ball can't roll under the furniture.

Cheaper cat-litter liners

• *A box* of ten plastic lawn bags makes forty litter-pan liners. Cut each bag into four large rectangular pieces.

 FINS AND FEATHERS

Cleaning fish tanks

• *Soap should* never be used to clean fish tanks. Use nylon netting and noniodized table salt. Rinse tank well to remove all residue.

When your bird flies the coop
• *Turn off* the lights and close the drapes. A bird will normally stay motionless in the dark until you can catch him.

Take a bath
• *Here's how* you coax birds into the birdbath: put some sand on the bottom, and a few seeds on the surface of the water.
• *And if* it's in the sun, move it to the shade. The water may get too warm.

There's a fungus among us
• *Get rid* of birdbath fungus. Soak some towels in bleach and place them on the sides of the empty bath for half an hour. Remove the towels (and rinse bath thoroughly).

PEST PROCEDURES

Bugging off
• *To prevent* flies from swarming around garbage pails, hose the cans down and allow to dry in the sun. Then, sprinkle a little dry soap in them.
• *Throw a* few mothballs in the garbage can to neutralize odors and keep out insects.

Keeping insects at bay
• *Several bay* leaves in a cupboard that has been thoroughly scrubbed are particularly effective against pests of all kinds. The leaves should be replaced after about a year.

• *A few* sticks of wrapped spearmint chewing gum placed on the shelf near open packages of noodles, macaroni, or spaghetti keep mealworms and other pests at a distance.

Hounded by dogs?
• *If stray* dogs are attacking the garbage, sprinkle full-strength ammonia over the garbage bags before placing them in the pail. (This will discourage insects as well.)

Ant-agonizers
• *To keep* ants out of the house, place whole cloves where they enter. And tuck a few in the corners of your kitchen cupboards and under a kitchen sink.
• *Ants are* also deterred by dried coffee grounds sprinkled around outside doors leading to the kitchen.
• *For a* lethal ant concoction, mix two cups of borax and one cup of sugar in a quart jar. Punch holes in the lid and sprinkle around outside foundation of the house.

There's a bee in the house
• *If a* wasp or bee gets into the house, reach for the hair spray. Most insect sprays only infuriate them, but the hair spray stiffens their wings, immobilizing them immediately. This works on all winged insects.

How to treat bug bites
• *Treat insect* bites with a poultice of either corn-starch or baking soda, mixed with vinegar, fresh lemon juice, or witch hazel.
• *Apply a* paste made of meat tenderizer and water.
• *Or, rub* bites with a wet bar of soap to help relieve itching.

Don't Mickey Mouse around

• *Mice can't* stand the smell of fresh peppermint. Put the sprigs in mouse-haunted places. Or saturate a piece of cardboard with oil of peppermint, available at most drugstores.

• *You can* trap mice with a piece of cotton soaked in lard or bacon grease. They like to eat lard and use the cotton for their nests. Tack the cotton to the bait pan of the trap.

• *Another good* mousetrap bait is peanut butter. It works much better than cheese.

Good riddance to roaches

Note: These hints are not for use in homes with small children and/or pets.

• *A one-pound* can of boric acid compound can effectively keep a house cockroach-free for a year. It will not kill roaches as rapidly as some pesticides, but it has by far the longest-lasting effect. (If they don't pick up a toxic dose of other pesticides in their first contact, roaches learn to stay clear. Boric acid, however, will not repel roaches, so they keep going back into it over and over until they die.) Simply sprinkle it in cracks, crevices, under sinks, and in other dark places. To be rid of them immediately, spray with a pesticide and after a few days start using the boric acid method.

• *Fill a* large bowl with cheap wine and set it under the sink. The roaches will drink it, get drunk, fall in, then drown. This is not a joke. It's been known to have great results.

• *Or place* a bowl of dry cement and a bowl of water next to each other . . . and guess what happens.

Silverfish
• *Sprinkle a* mixture of boric acid and sugar on affected areas.

Keeping squirrels out of a bird feeder
• *Cut a* hole in the bottom of a plastic wastebasket and slide it upside down on the pole that holds the feeder.

21

Best of Helpful Hints for Painting and Wallpapering

UP AGAINST THE WALL

Trying out a large paint sample
• *If you* have a hard time visualizing how a color will look on your walls, buy a small amount and paint a piece of sixteen-by-twenty-inch poster board with it. That is big enough to show how a color will look on larger areas. Move it around to various spots in the room and see how it looks under different kinds of light.

Keep a color-code record
• *On the* back of the light-switch plate, write down the color and amount of paint used in each room.

Small wallpaper patterns are better buys
• *Since you* want to match the pattern as you hang the paper, remember that a pattern that's repeated every eight inches means a lot less waste per roll than a pattern that's repeated every twenty-four inches.

DRIP-PROOFING

Dish it out
• *Use a* metal soup ladle and you can transfer latex paint from the can to the paint tray neatly.

Cover-ups
• *An old* pair of socks slipped over shoes protects them from paint splatters.
• *Keep a* couple of plastic sandwich bags handy to slip over hands if the doorbell or telephone rings.
• *Or, wrap* a rag around the telephone receiver and fasten it with rubber bands.

Tops for drops
• *When painting* the ceiling, you can prevent drops from landing on your head by simply sticking the paintbrush through the middle of a paper plate and securing with Scotch tape.
• *Before painting* a chair or table, place jar lids under each leg to catch paint drips.
• *Same goes* for stripper. You not only protect the floor, but you can reuse the excess stripper.
• *To prevent* drips of paint from falling on your light fixtures, tie plastic bags around them.

Shower curtain drop cloth
• *Save old* shower curtains. They're heavier and more durable than many plastic drop cloths that you buy.

ALL STIRRED UP

Lumpy paint
• *The best* strainer of all is an old nylon stocking.
• *An old* egg beater is excellent for stirring paint.
• *Cut a* circle from an old screen, slightly smaller than the can lid. As the screen settles, it will carry all lumps to the bottom.

Here's the drill
• *Several holes* drilled in the end of your paint paddle will make stirring easier.

BUCKET BRIGADE

A better paint bucket
• *A portable,* lightweight paint bucket can be fashioned from an empty, clean plastic milk or bleach bottle. Opposite the handle, cut a hole for the paintbrush to fit through easily.

Eliminating paint-can messes
• *Don't use* the side of the can to remove excess paint from your brush. Use a straight piece of wire coat hanger fastened across the opening of the can. To hold it in place, bend the wire at right angles, inserting the ends in two nail holes punched at opposite sides of the rim.
• *Or put* a heavy rubber band lengthwise around the can so the band divides the can in half and makes a "partition." Use the band to wipe excess paint off the brush. Sides and top of can stay nice and neat.

Pour it on
• *Before pouring* paint from a can, cover the rim with masking tape. After pouring, remove the tape: the rim will be clean and the cover will fit tightly.
• *Or, poke* holes around the inside of the rim with a hammer and nail so paint will drip back into the can.

SPECIAL TREATMENTS

Preventing white paint from yellowing
• *Stir a* drop of black paint into any good white paint.

Banishing paint odor
• *Add two* teaspoons of vanilla extract per quart of paint.
• *Place a* large pan of water that contains a tablespoon of ammonia in the freshly-painted room. Leave overnight.

Bugging off
• *Have you* ever been "bugged" by flies and other insects landing on a freshly painted outdoor surface? Try squirting some bug repellent into the paint before applying.

ODD JOBS

Closets
• *To brighten* dingy closets, paint with high-gloss white enamel.

Drawer knobs
• *Remove them* from the dresser and set them screw-end down into empty soda bottles. Spray paint or paint with a brush. No missed spots or painted fingers

Picture frames
• *Place a* long, narrow stick (like a yardstick) along the center back of the frame, and lightly tack it to the top and bottom. The stick should be at least a foot longer than the frame so you can hold the frame on it as if it were a paddle. Hold the frame by this "handle" to paint. When the frame is dry, pull off the handle. There'll be no damage to the frame.

Radiators
• *When painting* with enamel paint, be sure the radiators are warm so the finish will last longer. Warmth tends to bake paint on the metal. (Check to see that the paint is specified for use with radiators.)

Screens
• *Tack a* small piece of carpeting to a wood block and dip it in the paint. You'll use less paint, and it will spread quickly and evenly.

Stairways
• *You can* use your stairway while painting it. Paint every other step on one day, and the rest on the next.
• *If you're* painting basement steps, or other outdoor steps that you want to make less slippery, mix a little sand with the paint so steps will be a lot less slippery.

Windows
• *To eliminate* window scraping, try these tips: dampen strips of newspaper or any other straight-

edged paper with warm water. Spread strips around each windowpane, making sure that the paper fits tightly into corners and edges. The paper will cling until you have finished with the paint job.

• *Rub a* bar of softened soap around the windowpanes.

• *Or, swab* on liquid detergent with a paintbrush (a few inches from the frame). When the windows dry, paint away.

• *Before painting* windows, remove the hard-to-get dirt out of nooks and crannies with an old paintbrush.

• *Coat door* hinges, doorknobs, lock latches, and other hardware with a coating of petroleum jelly. This will eliminate a lot of scraping after.

Wrought iron
• *Use a* smooth piece of sponge. When the piece starts to get tacky, toss it and use a fresh one.

BRUSH WORK

Loosen up
• *Run a* comb through the paintbrush to pull out loose bristles before you start. Then they won't come off in the paint.

Stop and go
• *When working* on a paint job that takes a couple of days, save time by thoroughly wrapping brushes in several layers of foil and freezing (stick them right into the freezer compartment of your refrigerator). Let brushes defrost an hour or more before returning to the job.

Right ways to clean brushes

• *Never let* paintbrushes rest on their bristles in a can of solvent, because they will bend and lose their shape. Put solvent in an empty coffee can, cut an *X* in the plastic lid, and push the brush handle up through the slit. That way the brush will hang in the can.

• *There's a* way to clean several brushes at one time. Suspend them in the solvent from a piece of wire coat hanger slipped through the holes in the brush handles.

• *And to* clean small brushes, poke the handles through a piece of cardboard, then lay the cardboard over the top of a small can of solvent.

• *Give clean* brushes a pointed edge by hanging the bristles between clamp-type hangers.

Shake it off

• *The neatest* way to shake solvent out of your brush is to squeeze the top of a bag around the handle and shake the solvent into the bag.

A MATTER OF SPLATTERS

Spattered paint on windows

• *Use nail* polish remover. Allow to soak for a few minutes, then rub off with a cloth and wash with warm suds. The paint will usually disappear, no matter how long it has been there.

• *Soften old* stains with turpentine and scrape off with a razor blade. This method also works on putty stains.

• *Wash freshly-dried* paint off glass with a hot vinegar solution.

Cleaning the woodwork
• *Very fine*, dry steel wool will remove spatters from woodwork.

Spatters on tile and porcelain
• *Use a* pumice stick (available at hardware stores).

Hinges and door pulls
• *To get* paint and varnish off, simmer them for a few minutes in baking soda and water, then wipe off the solution with a rag.

IN THE CAN

Storing leftover paint
• *To prevent* scum forming on leftover paint, place a disc of aluminum foil directly on the paint surface. To make the disc the correct size, set the can on the foil and cut around it.
• *Keep oil-based* paint fresh by adding four table-spoons of mineral spirits only to the top layer of the paint. Do not mix until the next paint job.

Can do
• *When replacing* the lid on a can of paint, drape a cloth over the lid, then hammer the lid back on.
• *Or, tightly* fit the lids of paint containers and store upside down. Scum will not form on paint.
• *Always mark* the paint level and color on each can before storing.

• *Use nail* polish or shoe polish bottles for leftover paint (and label them!). They are excellent for small touch-ups.

PATCH WORK

Homemade compounds
• *On wallpapered* walls: All you need is a box of crayons. Soften the crayon tip over a match for a few seconds. Wipe it off with paper toweling before rubbing it into the hole. Two or more colors may have to be used to match unusual shades. Wait several minutes, then remove the excess color by rubbing gently with paper towels.
• *Patch with* equal parts salt and starch. Add enough water for a smooth surface.
• *Or, fill* hole with white toothpaste.
• *On woodwork:* Mix a little, dry instant coffee with spackling paste or starch and water. Smooth with a damp cloth.

An easy tip to avoid expensive plastering bills
• *If the* plaster is cracking on the ceiling, try this: Mix some Elmer's glue with baking soda, making a paste. Apply to cracks with fingers. This trick could help postpone replastering for months.

Take the hue
• *An easy* way to repair a hole in colored plaster is to mix paint or food coloring in the plaster (or one of the homemade compounds above) to match the color of the walls.

Substitute for spackle
• *Mix white* glue with finely shredded white facial tissue. Alternately add glue and tissues while kneading the mixture until it's puttylike in consistency.

Camouflaging hairline cracks on white walls
• *Make a* runny paste with equal parts of table salt and laundry starch powder mixed with water. Apply paste with a small artist's brush.

WALLPAPERING

Marking nail holes when wallpapering
• *Put a* finishing nail (the kind without a head) or a toothpick into the holes where pictures hang. As you come to these areas, push the nail through the paper.

A foolproof idea
• *If, like* most walls, yours are slightly uneven, dab the corners with a quick coat of paint of the same color as the wallpaper. This will hide any spots where the paper edges don't quite meet.

How to store leftover wallpaper
• *Store some* leftover scraps of wallpaper by stapling them to an attic wall. When you need to repair a worn spot, your patches will be just as faded as the paper on the wall.

PANELING

As great as it "seams"
• *Before you* install paneling, approximate where the seams will join and paint a matching stripe two inches wide. Later, if the seams separate, the old wall color won't show through.

CLEANUP TIME

Right at hand
• *Attach several* cup hooks to the top of a wooden ladder for rags and they'll be available when you need them.

Paint removers for face and hands
• *Cooking oil* or baby oil is a better way to remove paint than turpentine because it will not burn the skin.
• *For easy* removal, rub Vaseline on exposed skin.

Ways to clean rollers
• *Fill an* empty quart milk carton with solvent, put the roller inside, crimp the ends shut. Give the carton a few shakes, then let it sit for a couple of hours.
• *Or, use* a tennis-ball can.

Bag it
• *Put a* large plastic bag over your roller pan before putting the paint in. When you are through, throw the bag away.

Unclogging removable spray-paint nozzles
• *Keep a* tiny jar of paint thinner handy and drop each nozzle in after painting. Thinner stops the paint from clogging the tiny holes so they'll be clean and ready to use when you need to touch up something.

Ouchless stain remover
• *Remove varnish* stains from hands with an application of Spray 'n' Wash. Spray it on, rub hands, then wash with soap and water. In most cases it'll work better than turpentine, and it doesn't burn.

UP AGAINST THE WALL

Tools at hand
• *Wear a* carpenter's apron when wallpapering. You'll have all tools at hand so you won't have to run up and down the ladder retrieving them.

No-lump paste
• *Stir first* with a wire whisk. Gets rid of bubbles, too.

Tinted paste
• *Add a* bit of food coloring to wallpaper paste. It helps you see whether you've covered the paper to the very edge.

Paste substitutes for emergencies
• *Use an* egg white when wallpaper starts to pull away at the corners.

• *Or*, *try* gluing it back in place with some toothpaste.

• *Or*, *pull* the paper away from the wall as far as you can without tearing it. Brush an even, light coat of white household glue on the wall and on the paper and press it back onto the wall. Sponge off any excess glue, then run your fingers over the glued area for a minute or two.

Wallpapering behind the radiator
• *If the* radiator's a few inches from the wall, this will work great. Smooth the paper down as far as you can with the brush. Wrap a hand towel around a stick and poke it down behind the radiator, smoothing as you go.

Correcting an uneven edge
• *If your* wallpaper is uneven near the ceiling, cover with matching border paper.

Before repapering a wall
• *Cover all* grease spots with shellac and allow to dry thoroughly. This effectively prevents the grease spots from coming through on the new paper.

How much wallpaper?
• *Try this* formula to determine how many rolls of wallpaper will be needed to paper a room. Multiply the distance around the room (in feet) by the height of the room, then divide by thirty—if the pattern repeats every eighteen inches. Deduct one-half roll for every ordinary-sized opening such as windows and doors. The answer will equal the number of rolls needed. This allows for matching patterns.

Patching wallpaper
• *When you* are tearing (never cut) wallpaper to make a patch, tear toward the wrong side of the paper. The patch will be almost invisible.

Ballpoint-pen marks
• *Clean ballpoint-pen* marks off woodwork and painted walls with distilled white vinegar. First dab it on with a clean rag, then blot. Repeat as many times as necessary.
• *For wallpaper,* dampen the spot with water, then apply a very light coat of hair spray. Let it set a minute, then blot with a dry rag.

Removing unsightly bulges
• *Slit the* bulge with a razor blade. Using a knife, insert some paste under the paper. Smooth with a wet sponge.

Plaster with no lumps
• *If you* add plaster to water, instead of water to plaster, the mixture will be lump-free.

Another plaster tip
• *You can* slow the hardening of plaster by adding a little vinegar to the mixture.

How to hide nail holes from the landlady
• *Rub toothpaste* into the hole and smooth with a damp sponge.

A crack filler
• *Fill cracks* with steel wool or newspaper before finishing off with plaster.

Brushing away cobwebs
• *Slip a* sock or two over the end of a yardstick. Secure with a rubber band. Also good for cleaning under the refrigerator and radiators.

22

Best of
Helpful Hints
for Sewing and Knitting

YOU CAN BE SEW CLEVER

New sources for fabric
• *If nothing* tempts you at the yard goods store, check the fabrics in the home furnishing section of department stores.
• *Or check* the linen department.

How much fabric to buy?
• *To figure* out how much yardage you'll need, fold a sheet so it's the same width as the fabric you plan on using. Lay the pattern pieces out on it and measure.

Watch out for the table
• *Cover it* with a plastic tablecloth to protect it from scissors scratches. Since the scissors glide over the plastic, cutting will be easier too.

Don't confuse back and front
• *If you* cut front pattern pieces with a plain scissors and the back with a pinking shears, it'll be easier to match the pieces.

Storing fabric scraps
• *Take a* plastic garbage can with a lid. Tape a small sample of each piece of fabric to the lid. Now, when you need a certain type of fabric, you can check the lid instead of having to rummage through the whole can.

PRESSING MATTERS

Sharper creases in pants
• *Press creases* into each leg before sewing the pant leg together.

A new angle
• *If you're* making something that requires pressing after sewing each piece, make life simpler by putting your ironing board at right angles to your sewing machine. Adjust the board to your sitting height and you'll save time and energy.

I'VE GOT A NOTION

Scissors tips
• *Those rubber* tips used to cover the points of knitting needles are also great to protect points of small scissors. No more worry about jabbing your hand on them in the sewing basket.
• *Or,* you can store them in an eyeglass case.

Tweeze easy

• *Keep a* pair of tweezers in your sewing basket. It's great for pulling a needle through thick fabric.

• *Or*, use it to help you thread needles.

Storage in your sewing basket

• *Snaps: Snap* them together through a piece of cheesecloth.

• *Sequins: Tiny* plastic boxes from breath mints are perfect.

• *Trimming: Wind* remnants of bias binding, seam binding and lace around large-size empty thread spools and fasten ends down with masking tape.

Three cheers for Velcro fasteners

• *Velcro fasteners* are handy for fastening felt letters and emblems to cheerleaders' outfits. Emblems won't have to be removed and resewn every time you wash the garments, and one set of emblems can be used for several different uniforms.

HEMMING WAYS

Take the plunge

• *A sink* plunger is a handy gadget to use when making a skirt for hemming. Mark the handle at the desired length, then move the plunger around the hem. It stands by itself, leaving your hands free to mark or pin.

No time-wasting when basting

• *Mark the* hemlines with tailor's chalk, then use hair clips to hold the hem fold in place. Now you don't have to pin or baste at all, and there will be no pinhole in the fabric, either.

The best way to hem curtains

• *Shorten them* at the top instead of at the bottom. No one will notice if your job isn't perfect.

An ounce of prevention

• *When hemming* a slip or delicate fabric, make a knot in the thread every few inches. If the hem rips, you'll only have repairs between knots.

THREAD LINES

Perfect match

• *Before dyeing* a garment, baste a few strands of white thread through it. When finished, remove the threads and wrap them around a spool for future mending or hemming.

Smoother stitching

• *Pull the* thread over a piece of wax so the thread can slip through the material lots easier.

Fewer tangles with double thread

• *Put a* separate knot at the end of each thread.
• *Or run* thread over a sheet of fabric softener.

Eliminating the knot
• *When you* sew with a single thread, does it constantly knot? Then try this: After you thread the needle, be sure to knot the end that was cut off closest to the spool.

Rewinding a bobbin
• *Mark the* thread with contrasting color crayon a few yards after starting to wind it up. You'll know you're almost out of thread when the crayon mark comes up.

Recycling bobbin thread
• *Instead of* unwinding it and tossing out the thread so you can rewind the bobbin with another thread, wind the last bit of thread on an empty spool and use for hand-sewing.

Paired up
• *To keep* a bobbin and matching thread together, run a pipe cleaner through both, then twist.

ON PINS AND NEEDLES

Close at hand
• *Thread a* few needles with basic-colored thread and keep them in a safe, handy place near your washing machines. If you spot a loose hem or a small tear, fix it before you wash the item.

Threading a needle
• *Spray a* bit of hair spray or spray starch on your

finger when threading a needle and apply it to the end of the thread. The thread stiffens just enough to ease the job of finding the eye.

Sharpening a machine needle
• *Stitch through* a piece of sandpaper.

Handy pincushions
• *A bar* of soap makes an ideal place to stick needles and pins. It lubricates them so that they will go through stiff fabrics with ease.
• *Or stuff* a fabric square with one or two steel wool balls and sew closed. Your homemade pincushion holds pins and sharpens them, too.

Pin retrieval
• *A small* magnet glued to the end of a yardstick makes it easy to retrieve dropped pins and needles without having to bend.

RIGHT ON THE BUTTON

Storing buttons
• *When removing* buttons from a soon-to-be-discarded item, sew them together before storing with your spares. You'll save the time of having to match buttons later.

Getting in position
• *Keep the* buttons in place while you stitch: After positioning each button for a shirt, tape them onto the fabric with transparent tape.
• *Or use* a dot of white glue to hold each button in

place before sewing it on. The glue washes out of most fabrics easily. (To be safe, test glue on the reverse side first.)

These tricks are cute as a button

• *To keep* four-hole buttons on longer, sew through only two holes at a time, breaking the thread and knotting it for each pair of holes. Should one set break loose, the other side will hold the button.

• *When covering* a button with a sheer fabric, the job will be neater if you first cover the button with wool or flannel.

• *To avoid* cutting into the fabric when snipping off a button, slide a comb between the button and the cloth.

Repairing shank buttons

• *If the* shank of decorative buttons breaks off, sew a small flat button to the fabric, then glue the decorative button to it.

Buttonholes

• *Make sample* strips of different-sized buttonholes with an automatic buttonholer. Match the button to the sample size when trying to decide which size buttonhole to make.

• *Mark the* opening of handmade buttonholes with a thin coat of colorless nail polish. When the polish dries, snip the buttonhole open and get straight, nonraveling edges that are ready to stitch over.

• *When cutting* buttonholes by machine, mark the ends of the hole with straight pins to avoid cutting too far.

• *To hide* interfacing that shows along the edge of a buttonhole, color it with a marking pen to match the fabric.

• *Sew the* buttonholes horizontally when making children's clothing and they'll be less likely to pop open while kids play.

Buttonholing on heavy fabrics
• *To snip* open buttonholes on heavy fabric so they're straight, put a bar of soap under the buttonhole, and cut through with a single-edge razor blade.
• *Use single* strands of embroidery floss instead of thread when hand-stitching them.

Loose buttons
• *Touch the* center of the button (front and back) with clear nail polish if a button comes loose and you can't repair it right away.

ZIPPITY-DO

Bottom's broken
• *If zipper* teeth are broken near the bottom, sew that end closed and make the zipper a little shorter.

It won't stay closed
• *Sew a* small button at the top and make a loop of strong thread through the hole in the zipper pull. When you zip up, just hook the loop over the button.

Reusing a zipper
• *Spray it* heavily with spray starch and it will handle like new. Zippo!

ON THE MEND

Securing drawstrings

• *Tack the* drawstrings at the back center seam. String won't be swallowed up either one way or the other.

• *Or, sew* "balls" from a piece of ball fringe to the ends of drawstrings. That should keep them from slipping into the casing.

• *Or, sew* flat buttons to each end of the drawstring.

"Darn" it all

• *Stick a* straight wooden clothespin inside the finger of gloves that need mending.

• *A ragged* hole or tear will be easier to darn if you pull the fabric together as much as possible and iron it between two pieces of waxed paper.

• *Place a* thin sheet of paper under the hole in a garment and darn back and forth with the sewing machine. When the garment is washed, the paper will dissolve. This is ideal for bedsheets with big tears or rips.

• *To repair* a hole in a bulky-knit fabric, use the plastic L'Eggs pantyhose egg for a darning surface.

Let's patch things up

• *Get the* most wear out of your youngster's play pants by turning them inside out and ironing patches on the seat and knees.

A pocketful of sense

• *A piece* of cardboard placed inside the pocket when mending it prevents your needle from catching the other side.

• *Use the* same color material to make the pockets as that of the slacks. Unsightly white pocket lining won't show every time you sit.
• *When sewing* the pocket on a new garment, reinforce the top corners with a small piece of the fabric sewn on the inside.

Iron-on patching jeans

• *Trace around* cookie cutters for fun-shaped patches.
• *If a* worn-out patch needs replacing, remove it by pressing it with a hot iron. The patch should peel right off.

Make it snappy

• *Sew the* snap point on first. Then take a piece of chalk and touch this little point. Turn the material over, rub it with your finger, and you will find that you have marked the exact place where the snap should be sewed on.

TRICKS OF THE TRADE

Sewing on appliqués

• *If you* dip them first into a weak solution of cold starch, then press in place, they won't slip around as you sew them on. Starching keeps them from wrinkling, too.

For absolutely even stitches
• *Run the* fabric through a threadless sewing machine. Hand-stitch by following the tiny puncture holes.

Bibs from remnants
• *When making* dresses or tops for tots, use the scraps to sew up matching bibs. Trim with bias tape or lace to match.

You'll deserve a badge
• *Use a* few dabs of any good white glue on the back of the emblem and press it in position on the clothing, then let it set for a few minutes. The emblem can then be stitched by hand (or machine) without any worry that it will turn out lopsided. The glue subsequently washes out.

Sewing on plastic
• *Put wax* paper over the seam and the sewing machine will not stick to the plastic, nor pucker. The wax paper will tear off easily after the job is done.

Slip-sliding away?
• *To sew* hard-to-handle fabrics like nylon tricot or crepe, put a piece of brown paper bag or notebook paper under them and sew through both thicknesses. Stitch through the fabric and paper (and you won't skip stitches). When finished, tear the paper off.
• *And, delicate* fabrics won't slip off your lap while you're working on them if you wear a terry cloth apron.
• *Slide-proof a* satin quilt or comforter by sewing a piece of muslin across the bottom and tucking that

part under the mattress. It won't slide around the bed anymore.

For worn elastic
• *Whenever elastic* that is sewn on a garment becomes worn or stretched, just baste cord elastic through the worn elastic. Pull it up and knot.

FOLLOWING A PATTERN

Storing patterns
• *Your favorite* patterns will last longer if you put them in manila envelopes or locking plastic bags.
• *The cut-out* pieces of a pattern will stay smoother if you hang them on a clamp-type skirt hanger instead of folding them.

Repairing patterns
• *Use a* strip of plastic freezer paper to repair a torn pattern. Place a torn section over the freezer paper and press with a warm iron.

Homemade patterns
• *Look through* a children's coloring book for simple, decorative outlines for quilt patterns.
• *Use a* coloring book that features your youngster's favorite movie or television character to make a novelty print for a T-shirt or pajama top. Trace the picture onto the garment with tracing carbon, then color it in with ballpoint fabric paint (available at craft stores).
• *The peel-away* backings from adhesive shelf paper,

which are ruled in one-inch squares, make handy
guides for enlarging your needlework patterns.

NEEDLE LITTLE KNITTING HELP?

No more yarn tangles
• *Make your* own yarn holder with a liter-sized plastic
soda bottle. Carefully remove the plastic piece that
fits on the bottom of the bottle. Cut the bottom off the
bottle, insert a full skein of yarn, then thread it up
through the top. Snap the plastic bottom back on.
• *Or, when* working with several colors of yarn at
once, thread each through a different drinking straw
to keep ends from getting tangled.
• *Or, pry* the top off a cleaner can like Comet, then
wash and dry the top. Pull the end of each color yarn
through one hole in the top.

Marking a stitch
• *Here's a* quick and easy marker: cut a one-eighth-
inch slice off a plastic drinking straw. The straw rings
fit right on knitting needles up to size ten.
• *Or, try* using a twist tie. It's easy to transfer from
needle to needle and works just as well as expensive
plastic markers.

Stitch-holder substitutes
• *Single bar-type* barrettes are great for this.
• *Or, use* a metal shower curtain ring.
• *Or, use* safety pins but put a small button on the pin
first so yarn doesn't get caught on the spring end.

Keeping stitches on the needles
• *When you* lay work aside, wind a rubber band tightly around the tips of the needles and tuck the first stitch under it for safekeeping.
• *Or, press* small corks on the tips.

Sewing a sweater together
• *Instead of* attaching the pieces with straight pins, use plastic picks that come with hair rollers. They're much longer, stronger, and won't get lost in the sweater.

Fringe benefits
• *Double the* number of fringes you make at one time by winding yarn around a magazine lengthwise instead of a smaller object. Cut yarn top and bottom, then double over each bunch to make a fringe.

Storing large quantities of yarn
• *Use liquor* cartons with compartment dividers. Color or types of yarn can be kept separately.

23

Best of
Helpful Hints
for Travel

LET'S GET PACKING

Do-it-yourself travel kits

• *Fill a* plastic egg-shaped pantyhose container with your jewelry. It's compact and closes tightly so contents won't spill out into suitcase.

• *Turn an* empty 35-mm film canister into a nifty sewing kit. Insert a few buttons, bobbins of thread, needles, safety pins, and so on.

• *Protect cosmetics* and small bottles by putting them in a small plastic lunchbox to tuck in your luggage.

Packing an airtight case

• *When packing* shampoo, mouthwash, and liquid cosmetics in plastic bottles, squeeze the bottle and force out some of the air just before tightening the cap. This creates a partial vacuum and helps prevent leakage.

• *Make a* handy toothbrush container from a plastic pill bottle. Cut a slit in the top, slide the handle through it, and snap it back on the bottle with the bristles inside.

• *Instead of* traveling with a bottle of nail-polish remover, which might leak in your suitcase, saturate several cotton balls with the remover and keep them in a small, airtight jar.

Medical standbys

• *If you're* taking prescription drugs, pack enough for your trip.

• *Make sure* pills are in the original containers. Also, carry a copy of the prescription (written in its generic name, to make things easier in a foreign country) in case you need a refill or have some explaining to do at customs.

• *If you* combine two kinds of pills in one bottle to save space, label the bottle to remember which is which.

• *Take along* a supply of your contraceptives. In certain countries they might not be available.

• *You might* not have broken a pair in the last twenty years, but be sure to take along an extra pair of glasses or contact lenses, as well as your prescription. You don't want to remember the Eiffel Tower or the Taj Mahal as one big blur.

Storing suitcases

• *To keep* suitcases smelling fresh, store them with a fabric-softener sheet or a bar of scented soap inside.

• *Or put* a small packet of activated charcoal (available at your florist) inside.

• *Or use* crumpled-up newspaper to avoid musty odors.

EASY HANDLING

Case closed
• *Identification tags* that hang on the outside of the case can come off easily. For additional protection, place your name and address (use your business card, if you've got one) inside the liner of the suitcase. Also tape one on the outside. Cover it completely with tape so it can't be pulled off.
• *Tote bags* will travel better if you tie both handles together with twine. The bag will be less likely to rip open during handling.

Spot your luggage quickly
• *Wrap brightly* colored electrical tape around the handle.
• *Or tie* on some colorful yarn.

 AIR "LINES"

Baggage checks
• *Put identification* tags on both the outside and inside of suitcases. Bags without outside tags will be opened after three days if they haven't been claimed.
• *Most lost* luggage is checked in less than a half hour before flight time. So check in early.

'Ear ye, 'ear ye
• *Try a* medication like Ornade, Sudafed Plus, or a nose spray like Afrin or Neo-Synephrine about one and a half hours before descent to relieve those pains in your ears during landing.

• *Or, cover* your ears with plastic cups containing towels or napkins moistened with hot water.

If flying gets you in the stomach

• *If your* stomach bothers you in planes, it's because decreased atmospheric pressure at high altitudes causes gases to expand. So avoid gas-producing foods, avoid carbonated drinks, eat slowly, and stay away from gum (except during takeoff and landing, when chewing gum helps unstop your ears).

Legs aching on a long flight?

• *Try doing* knee raises right in your seat. Pull one knee up toward your chest, then lower it to the floor. Repeat a dozen times with each leg.

Avoiding airsickness

• *Fly after* dark.
• *Get seats* away from the engine and toward the center of the plane.
• *Ride in* a reclining position.

Inspections

• *If you* are traveling with a gift-wrapped package, wrap the lid and the box separately so the lid can be removed for inspection at the airport. (Use rubber bands to hold the lid on.)

Cameras

• *When taking* new, expensive, foreign-made cameras, watches, and records out of the United States, record them with U.S. Customs before you leave. This way, you can't be asked to pay duty on them when you return.

ROAD "WAYS"

Avoiding motion sickness

• *Children are* less likely to get carsick if they can see out the front window of the car.

• *Stay near* the center of a boat, close to the water level, or out on deck. Lie down with eyes open.

• *Or, try* sucking on a lemon for seasickness.

• *If you* feel airsick, look at a point on the distant horizon. This helps decrease the perception of motion.

For the long-distance driver

• *Researchers have* found that drivers who take a break for a hearty meal have better reaction times than those who don't.

• *If you* want to avoid back problems, be sure you don't have to stretch for the pedals. Adjust your car seat properly, and sit back.

• *If you* drive a lot, invest in a firm, flat backrest.

Saving space and trouble

• *Pack bedding* in drawstring laundry bags. The bags hold a lot without taking up much space, and they can double as pillows in the backseat for the kids.

• *You won't* have to empty the whole trunk to get to the jack (or other emergency equipment) if you pack it last.

For fast cleanups

• *Fill a* plastic liquid-detergent bottle (without rinsing it out) with water and keep it in the glove compartment, with paper towels.

Wish you were here
• *If you* plan to send postcards while on vacation, before you go put all the addresses on sticker labels instead of carrying your address book.

HOME AWAY FROM HOME

Don't forget these if you're staying in a hotel
• *A long* extension cord. It won't matter then where the mirror or outlets are in the room.
• *High-wattage* light bulb. Just in case you need more light when applying makeup or reading.
• *Water heater* and instant coffee or tea. No more waiting for (and paying for!) room service.
• *Several clip-type* clothespins for clipping slacks and skirts to ordinary hangers.

24

Best of Helpful Hints for Windows, Curtains, and Drapes

WASHING THE WINDOWS

The best homemade window cleaner
• *Add one-half* cup of ammonia, one-half cup of white distilled vinegar, and two tablespoons of cornstarch to a bucket of warm water for a perfect window-washing solution.

It's a stretch
• *To reach* high windows without a ladder, use a painter's pod on an extension pole.

Do 'em in gloom
• *Never wash* windows on sunny days. They will dry too fast and show streaks.

For fast cleanups
• *Wash with* a cloth soaked in white vinegar. This method is great when washing only a few indoor windows.

Here's some "news"
• *Shine with* newspaper instead of paper towels. It is cheaper and, some feel, easier. Be sure you have read the papers or the project could take all day.

Up and down, back and forth
• *No more* guesswork: When drying the inside panes with vertical strokes and the outside panes with horizontal strokes, or vice versa—you will notice quickly which side has the smudges.

For stubborn spots
• *Spray glass* with oven cleaner. Leave it there for a few minutes before wiping grime away.

Buff them up
• *After windows* have dried, rub a clean blackboard eraser over them for a really fine shine.

To avoid removing drapes
• *When washing* inside windows, put drapes through a clothes hanger and hang them from the curtain rod. Drapes will be safely out of the way.

Spotted sills
• *Pour a* little diluted rubbing alcohol on a soft cloth and rub the entire surface. Spots will not only disappear, but sills will look freshly painted.

FOR WINDOW "PANES"

Hiding window gates
• *Window gates* may keep you safe, but they're not the greatest-looking additions to a room. So paint them white to make them look like garden lattice-work. Place pots of morning glories or other climbing plants on the windowsill and train them to grow around the gates.
• *Or hang* café curtains on the bottom half of the window.

Noise relief
• *Stop window* rattles! Glue corn pads to the window frames.

Non-shattering news
• *To remove* a broken windowpane safely, glue newspaper to both sides of the glass, let it dry, then gently chip away the putty. The pane will come out without scattering glass splinters.
• *To loosen* an old pane of glass, pass a red-hot poker slowly over the old putty.

Removing decals
• *Soak with* warm water, peel off what you can, then get the remaining sticky residue off with nail polish remover.
• *Or use* salad oil.
• *Or saturate* with lighter fluid. (*Caution: It's flam-mable. Wash off all traces of lighter fluid after the sticker is off.*)

The hole story
• *Repair a* small hole in a windowpane by filling it with clear shellac or nail polish. Put a few drops in the hole and let dry; repeat as necessary until the hole is filled.

Before puttying windows
• *Mix putty* with the paint that matches the woodwork.

To prevent freezeups
• *During winter,* add one-half cup of rubbing alcohol or anti-freeze to each quart of water you use for cleaning windows.

If windows are ice-covered
• *Rub with* a mixture of one-half cup of rubbing alcohol or anti-freeze per each quart of water used.
• *Or just* rub the inside of windows with a sponge that has been dipped in rubbing alcohol or antifreeze. Polish with paper towels or newspaper.
• *Or rub* with a cloth moistened with glycerin, leaving a little of the glycerin on the inside of the glass.
• *Or, head* south.

BLIND ALLEYS

Anti-static device
• *Wipe mini-blinds* or vertical blinds with damp fabric softener sheets to eliminate static that collects dust. The same trick works for your TV screen.

Washing techniques
• *When blinds* are really dirty, hang them on a clothesline and hose them down.
• *Or hang* them under the shower.

Miniblind cleaner
• *A cloth* saturated with rubbing alcohol and wrapped around a rubber spatula will easily reach into tiny slats.

To keep tapes from puckering
• *Venetian blind* tapes will be less likely to pucker or shrink when washed if you secure them top and bottom with adhesive-backed tape while they dry.

For broken tape
• *Tape the* side that faces the wall with heavy-duty packing tape. Apply white canvas shoe polish.

When tape is dirty
• *Brighten up* the tape with white shoe polish applied with a damp sponge.

CURTAIN TIME

Great body
• *You can* eliminate most of the ironing after washing Dacron curtains: add one packet of unsugared gelatin, dissolved in plain hot water, to the final rinse water.
• *Freshen them* in the dryer with a fabric softener sheet and a damp towel.

Rinse secret
• *Kitchen curtains* will hold their body and require less ironing if one-half cup of Epsom salts is added to the final rinse water when washing.

Disguising curtain rods
• *Take the* rods down, wash them off, and paint them as near the color of the window molding as possible, being careful not to get too much paint on the cords of the traverse rods.

Preventing rip-offs
• *Cut the* finger of an old glove to cover your curtain-rod end before slipping it through delicate curtains.
• *Or use* a plastic bag.

Easy-moving curtain rods
• *After washing* traverse or curtain rods, wax them. They will move much better. This applies to new rods as well.

Are your tiebacks straight?
• *A foolproof* way to get tiebacks straight across from each other when hanging curtains is to use your window shade as a measuring guide.

SCREEN TESTS

For small jobs
• *Rub a* brush-type hair roller lightly over the screen and see how easily it picks up all the lint and dust.

Bigger jobs . . .

• *Clean screens* with the dusting attachment of a vacuum cleaner.
• *Or brush* with carpet scraps that have been nailed to a wood block.

Biggest jobs . . .

• *To be* really thorough, brush on both sides with kerosene. Wipe with a clean cloth. This method will also prevent rust from forming. Be sure to dust the screens with a small paintbrush before you begin.

Jet cleaner

• *Take hopelessly* dirty screens to a do-it-yourself car wash. The high-pressure hoses shooting streams of hot, soapy water will clean off all dirt and grime.

Patch work

• *How do* you fix holes in a screen? For small holes, dab them with clear nail polish. Use thin coats to prevent drips.
• *Or, use* a few drops of airplane glue.
• *For larger* holes, cut a patch from a piece of old screen and glue the edges in place with airplane glue.

DRAPE EXPECTATIONS

Pulling the right cord

• *Stop guessing* which cord opens the pull drapes. Wrap a half-inch piece of clear tape about eye level around the right cord. It won't interfere with the pulleys.

Easy wrinkle remover
• *Remove wrinkles* from draperies: Spray them with a fine-mist plant sprayer as they hang.

Inserting drapery hooks
• *A soap* coating will make drapery hooks much easier to push into the fabric.

SHADY SUGGESTIONS

To mend a tear
• *On small* tears, colorless nail polish works wonders.

If shades can't be washed
• *Rub unwashable* shades with a rough flannel cloth that has been dipped in flour or corn meal.
• *A soft* eraser may remove spots and stains.
• *Or, buy* kneadable wallpaper cleaner for spot removal.

Parchment shade protection
• *Keep them* clean by waxing them.

INDEX